✄✄✄✄✄✄✄✄✄✄✄✄✄✄✄✄✄✄

Alternatives to the Traditional

How Professors Teach and How Students Learn?

✄✄✄✄✄✄✄✄✄✄✄✄✄✄✄✄✄✄

OHMER MILTON

ALTERNATIVES
TO THE
TRADITIONAL

Jossey-Bass Inc., Publishers

San Francisco • Washington • London • 1972

ALTERNATIVES TO THE TRADITIONAL
How Professors Teach and How Students Learn
by Ohmer Milton

Copyright © 1972 by Jossey-Bass, Inc., Publishers

Published and copyrighted in Great Britain by
Jossey-Bass, Inc., Publishers
3, Henrietta Street
London W.C.2

Library of Congress Catalogue Card Number LC 72-83961

International Standard Book Number ISBN 0-87589-138-1

Manufactured in the United States of America

JACKET DESIGN BY WILLI BAUM

FIRST EDITION

Code 7223

The Jossey-Bass
Series in Higher Education

Consulting Editor

HAROLD L. HODGKINSON
University of California, Berkeley

Preface

$\mathcal{A}$lthough extensive research about learning has been documented in innumerable publications, many faculty do not have the time, the familiarity with its specialized language, or the inclination to avail themselves of the literature. My contention is, however, that even elementary principles of learning, especially in higher education, have been neglected, abandoned to an abiding faith in traditional methods, or periodically subjected to innovative hunches. It is research that can guide us out of the overgrown thicket of dogma which surrounds current ideas about instruction and learning.

Preface

Faculty members are not alone in their support of dogma about teaching-learning. Students and the public-at-large are all too willing to advance explanations about what is wrong with instruction and to offer panaceas for its improvement. This is true because all of us have been in school and have had certain successes and failures there, a fact which lets us slide easily into confusing cause-effect relationships. Limited personal perceptions, however, suffice no longer as reliable guides for improvement.

Thus the predominating theme of *Alternatives to the Traditional* is an examination of learning research and selected academic practices toward the end, primarily, of inspiring new questions about arrangements for learning—questions which are entirely too belated in coming. The technical jargon of statisticians and researchers has been avoided assiduously, and, for the most part, my specific personal opinions, explanations, and solutions have been minimized.

While *Alternatives to the Traditional* is beamed especially to faculty members because they are the ones who can aid the cause of learning most directly, it is pointed also toward the increasing numbers of trustees, legislators, and other citizens making well-intentioned but sometimes ill-founded decisions which are affecting profoundly the course of higher learning. Concerned parents and students may profit as well because of the constant emphasis upon questions about learning and reminders that the promotion of learning has often been overlooked in much of the recent rhetoric. Students will suffer most if different questions are not asked.

Admittedly, research evidence is hard to obtain about many of the teaching-learning problems which plague higher education, but over the long haul the search is worth the effort, for objective data do provide a far better catapult for serious deliberation and experimentation than does mere personal opinion.

Several studies are mentioned which were conducted at the University of Tennessee by the following members of the faculty: Peggy S. Berger, J. H. Carruth, Harold J. Fine and Robert G. Wahler, James W. Hilty, Kelly Leiter, Anand Malik, M. W. Milligan and R. L. Reid, Max A. Robinson, Roger Rusk, Ronald R. Schmoller, William S. Verplanck, and Robert L. Williams.

Knoxville, Tennessee
August 1972

OHMER MILTON

Contents

Contents

Alternatives to the Traditional

How Professors Teach
and How Students Learn?

You cannot teach a man anything;
you can only help him to find it
within himself.

Galileo

1

❄❄❄❄❄❄❄❄❄❄❄❄❄

Probing the Faith

❄❄❄❄❄❄❄❄❄❄❄❄❄

Many of the ideas explored in this book are, in one sense, objectively and impersonally based; in another sense, they are quite subjective and have very personal roots. This contrast in origin stems partly from a sobering experience which occurred, at my unwitting instigation, about midway in my teaching career, when the several results of a little classroom exercise were totally unanticipated. The intellectual and emotional conflicts aroused in me at the time about teaching and the future role of faculty members in the classroom and in the curriculum have not yet been resolved. Because of this mental disequilibrium, many of the current proposals for needed changes and so-called innovations strike me as being singularly deficient and, most seriously, questioned only casually. Traditional, and in some cases ancient, conceptions about numerous matters continue to dominate many suggestions for reform and most research in higher education instruction. From time to time, philosophies and practices appropriate for the primary grades are copied for undergraduates. It is as though answers are being sought to issues about which the proper questions have not yet been conceived.

During the first half of some twenty years in the classroom, I possessed the all-too-common and seldom challenged exaggerated notions which many faculty members have about professorial influences on young adults. Judging by many of the recommendations for colleges and universities made by nonacademicians, I think the notions are shared widely. My observations of my teaching revealed not only that students clearly enjoyed my classes and were exhilarated by them but that their interests in the esoteric aspects of psychology were enhanced, that they developed a genuine spirit of scientific inquiry about human behavior, that they integrated data from psychology with data from other academic disciplines, and, perhaps most important of all, that they learned to reason or to think critically about all problems both at that time and forevermore. These qualities were fully promoted during only one academic quarter of thrice-per-week, fifty-minute meetings with me; all the while most of the students were being affected similarly, according to legend, by four colleagues in as many separate classes. This little vignette portrays at least one set of historical forces which continues to be awkwardly predominant in the teaching-learning arena and which decidedly limits alterations.

2

Probing the Faith

In the late 1950s, for reasons I do not recall at the moment but probably because research in the teaching-learning field was beginning to be respectable (that is, foundation money was becoming available and credit could be earned toward the publish or perish ratio), I attempted to gather evidence which would *support* my pretentious beliefs about my classroom performance. Consequently, it was so arranged that one group of introductory psychology students did not attend class for an entire quarter; they were provided with the full armamentaria for learning, such as syllabi and textbooks. At the same time, students in a companion section received the most exquisitely designed and executed instruction ever beamed to any group; all the exhortations which have been made through the ages about how to teach were followed assiduously three times per week. No classroom group has ever before heard such clear and *relevant* explanations of uniquely difficult concepts, been so stimulated, witnessed such enthusiasm, or, in essence, had as much personal "personal contact."

My psychic and visceral traumas began with the initial inspection of test data at the end of the quarter—the no-class group had performed slightly better than had the students in class. Furthermore, on successive and different measures gathered over a two-year period, the overall record of the no-class group was somewhat better than that of the attenders. A few more of the nonattenders took additional courses in psychology; about the same number chose to be psychology majors; and fewer of them withdrew from the university (while others may see cause-effect relationships here, I am still reluctant to do so!).

Student reactions in the no-class group were mixed. Around half expressed considerable resentment on a postcourse questionnaire about having been deprived of my countenance. The other half made such troubling comments as: "For the first time in my fourteen years in school, I found that I could

3

learn on my own—I *liked* the experience." One student who had surely gained in critical thinking ability offered the prize evaluation: "I have enjoyed the course and it has required little study time; however, *I am not doing exceptionally well.*" (Emphasis *not* added.)

As research goes, many valid criticisms can be made of the study, and I am personally familiar with all the Freudian rationalizations as well as the Hawthorne Effect,* which, at the time, "explained" what happened. Despite the manifest weaknesses, however, important conclusions can be drawn from the research, and those conclusions have plagued my thinking since then. In the event the reader wishes to reject the findings with "But in my classes, it's different," he must be forewarned that numerous studies in other disciplines tend to corroborate my results. I have terminated many professorial arguments about my findings with "Why don't you try such a study?" Few antagonists have accepted the challenge.

The considerable emotional coloring which pervades the thinking of most of us about instruction is at the root of much of the current confusion in higher education circles. This coloring is illustrated dramatically by an episode which occurred during collegiate evaluation of students in the famous Eight-Year Study (Chamberlin, Drought, and Scott, 1942). The experimental students, who had graduated from experimental high schools, were matched carefully for comparison purposes on the basis of several criteria with students who had graduated from conventional high schools: "A university professor was asked to report on five students in this Study who were enrolled in his class. He launched at once on a tirade

---

* The principle derives from a study conducted in the early 1930s at the Hawthorne Plant of the Western Electric Company. The effects of working conditions upon productivity were being investigated; it was found that the workers were more affected by the "experiment" than by specific working conditions.

4

against their poor performance. . . . According to him, they had never learned to read, couldn't write, couldn't spell, were always talking out of turn, couldn't concentrate, didn't know what work was, were always turning work in late if at all, and in general had no discipline. . . . His temper was not improved when he was informed that all five of the students involved had come from conventional schools and were members of the comparison group" (p. 22).

This remarkable distorting of cause-effect relationships, maintenance of predetermined perceptions, and adamant refusal to consider the interminable number of factors which influence learning continue to be prevalent. I maintain that wholesale faith in the traditionally acclaimed determinants of college learning is impeding solutions to very real and difficult problems; efforts must be made to sort out the myths and fantasies for public scrutiny and debate. Three hundred years of higher education instruction do not seem to be providing much sound guidance at the moment. Such historical forces may be compounded by our personal experiences in college as well as our school experiences prior to that. To speculate about these possibilities would take us too far afield; suffice to say, the no-class study truly modified (colored) my thinking.

Despite the inadequacies of my classroom exercise, at least one signal conclusion precipitated by it has hounded me: Better teaching in the classroom, as that activity is ordinarily conceived, is not the crucial issue in higher education. This conclusion is firmer now than it was initially as a result of my careful perusal of the research literature (see Chapter Two) and continued experimentation in my teaching. A second significant conclusion, by inference, is that the individual instructor working in isolation from and at variance with his colleagues is relatively ineffectual in his impact upon students. He is, after all, only one-fourth or one-fifth of the professorial total at any one time; moreover, numerous factors other than academic ones impinge upon students. The advice of the sages on teaching, which is paraded constantly, has been found wanting here in the last half of the twentieth century; indeed, one major investigator (Siegel, 1968) of the academic scene remarks: "Prescriptions for 'how to teach effectively' are about as outdated as leeching" (p. 144).

Instruction in its very broadest sense (and note I use "teaching" sparingly) is such a complex activity that it is difficult to know how best to proceed in developing evidence to support my signal conclusion. So many factors are inextricably bound together that to discuss one in isolation from others is to grossly oversimplify and invite invalidity. For these reasons I have not cataloged the various aspects of instruction too precisely. This chapter is designed to set the stage by touching globally upon basic issues in higher education instruction. My intent is to present ideas in such a manner that the reader will not look for answers; rather, a tone of spirited inquiry will be created. Progress in the promotion of learning is much more likely to result from new questions than from inherited answers.

If higher education is to be improved, the one issue which must be focused upon above all others is that students and their mentors seem to have basic misperceptions about learning. Both sets of participants take part in learning as though it were something imparted by the teacher to the learner. It is as though the teacher is supposed to "learn" the student. I believe that, in the thinking of many, this transmittal of learning from one person to another is mainly through spoken words. For hundreds of years a student and teacher absolutely had to be in the same place at the same time because the only way to dispense information was by mouth to nearby ears; the notion that teaching is talking is a historic carry-over from which higher education is only beginning to rumble about sundering itself. I do not have extensive data about what professors do in classrooms today (although ample anecdotal data are supplied by students) as evidence in support of my assertion about talking. In one study (Evans, 1962), however, 319 faculty members (all who responded from a total of 400) in one university ranked lectures as the most used and most favored teaching technique. They also believed the conveying of content was their most important contribution to learning (more about this in Chapter Two). In another study in a medium-sized university, Gruber and Weitman (1962) found essentially no difference between the number of hours freshmen and seniors spent in classrooms *listening* to the instructor—in arts and sciences as well as in engineering courses.

How about recording the time you do the talking in your classes? You may be surprised.

As might be expected, students have been conditioned to the fact that the role of the instructor is almost entirely one of conveying information in the classroom; he may also make assignments and test occasionally. Put another way, the instructor is to cover the material and explain the textbook. The "good" teacher, then, is one who performs those tasks well and spends most of his time at *only* those tasks. In completing a questionnaire about me in wake of the experimental class, one student wrote: "I cannot rate you because I have never *heard* you teach." In this setting, the student role is one of listening and *re*producing content on demand. One dissatisfied instructor (Hutchison, 1968) describes this sanctified route to learning thusly: "Students . . . must run around to fifteen lectures a week to hear their textbooks summarized" (p. 44).

One explanation for the endurance of this talking-listening strategy is certain assumptions that are made about the nature of learning. These assumptions have dominated instruction for hundreds of years and at least one of them originated prior to the coming of Christ (see Chapter Two). Academic practices on most campuses indicate that the assumptions seem to have been modified not at all by research about learning or by advances made during this century in knowledge about the structure and functioning of the brain. Maier (1971) summarizes these assumptions in this fashion: Education is essentially a process of accumulating information; proper instruction promotes the acquisition or learning of proper information; information once learned is, in effect, stored up and used later in problem solving; and there is a direct relationship between knowledge and action. Numerous studies cited later reveal the falsity of these notions when they are taken as being all inclusive.

One outgrowth of the talking-listening approach is that ultimately the instructor role becomes one of surveillance. Students must be cajoled and threatened, and a variety of ways must be devised to get them to study. The tragedy is that four years of college more often than not only strengthen the prior conditioning. Thousands of insightful faculty members will testify, too, that any departures from pushing and checking procedures provoke such resistance from the majority of students that they (the faculty), being thus thwarted, quickly return to the old, the familiar, and the comfortable. Still other faculty members maintain the surveillance role because they believe they should take stringent steps to prevent students from wasting taxpayers' (or philanthropists') money. Other well-meaning, dedicated professors insist they must cover the material compulsively because, to them, it is absolutely imperative that students master all the content of a particular course; and if they are to do so, students *cannot* be left to their own devices. Frankel (1959) observes: "In comparison to European students, American students seem to be more closely supervised, more elaborately protected, more vigorously exercised, and more solemnly prayed over" (p. 150).

Frequent proclamations about the need to improve teaching at the college level have been made as though a direct and absolute correlation exists between the *classroom* activities and behavior of the instructor and the learning of the students. In the thinking of many persons, improvement appears to mean that more professors should devote more time to the conveying of information and its related surveillance role. For example, in a survey (Milton, 1970) of almost three hundred adults (not connected with formal education), the following percentages agreed with each of these statements.

Professors should have absolute control over all activities in the classroom.	86%
All changes in a student's academic program, such as the dropping and adding of courses, should require the signature of the student's faculty advisor.	83
Generally, class attendance should be required and the roll should be checked at each meeting.	83
Learning on the college campus would be facilitated if there were regular homework assignments and if the students were questioned about it at the next class meeting.	64
Faculty members should lower a student's final course grade for an excessive number of class cuts.	59

This current support of the surveillance role appears to be part of the *in loco parentis* syndrome, which originated in Roman law well over two thousand years ago (Milton, 1970). The notion migrated to the United States via the legal system of England, and court decisions supported it prior to the turn of the century. The decree cited most frequently as having entrenched the doctrine was that of a Kentucky court in 1913 (Blackwell, 1961): "College authorities stand *in loco parentis* concerning the physical and moral welfare and mental training of students" (p. 104). While the concept is dying

9

legally for nonacademic aspects of student existence, it seems to continue to flourish for academic affairs. Note that the Kentucky court decision included mental training as part of the *in loco parentis* stance. Thus, selected aspects of instruction for young adults have been legalized.

With all our concern for surveillance and classroom activities in general, we have lost sight of the fact that learning, or better yet "to learn"—learning has been used so much as a noun, we seem to have forgotten that it is an active verb—is an individual, internal, and personal activity; no one person can learn for another. In the final analysis, learning occurs within the learner, and responsibility for learning can reside only in him. In a slightly different vein, Kestin (1963) comments: "When we think about the problems of higher education, we are too often carried away by the frequent use of the active verb 'to teach.' With very few exceptions, students are not taught by their professors in any direct sense. Teaching is not the transfer of knowledge or understanding from the brain of the instructor to a number of brains which belong to students. A higher education must be acquired by learning. Achievement in learning is the result of an intensive solitary struggle of each individual with himself" (p. 437).

The fact is that learning is both a process and a product; confusion results when the two functions are viewed interchangeably. The learning process refers fundamentally to the functioning of the nervous system, especially the brain, and need be of no direct concern to an instructor. It also refers to activities in which presumably a learner must engage, for example, repetition. I add "presumably" because repetition is necessary for some students, but it is not necessary for all. As a product, learning is a hypothetical construct; that is, on the basis of changes in the behavior of the learner, an observer infers that learning has taken place. When the small child, for example, manipulates the symbols $2 + 2 = ?$ correctly, or according to the rules of arithmetic, more or less consistently over a long period of time either orally or in writing, we judge that learning has occurred; more or less permanent change is the goal. Although in college the emphasis is upon a higher order learning, we are seeking more or less permanent changes in that realm also.

Perhaps the question "What must the learner do in order 'to learn'?" should be pondered to a much greater degree than it has been; that is, thoughtful deliberation is needed about learning as a process. (I am convinced, tentatively at least, that learning activities in a small child are different from those of a college student or young adult. Failure to consider that possibility, at any rate, may be one of the substantive problems in higher education.) Teaching, however, emphasizes what the instructor does—not what the student must do. Once we know the latter, the former should be evident.

While the professoriate has been urged to listen to students, have students really identified the important ingredients in learning?

By way of illustration of the uncertain soundness of college instructional practices, how does one explain the results of the following unreported study conducted on our campus— a study in which practice and feedback were manipulated as variables? One section of approximately twenty *junior* level mechanical engineering students in a course on conduction and radiation heat transfer received regular homework assignments which they were required to complete; these were corrected more carefully than usual by a coinstructor and were returned to them. Students in a comparison section of the same size and taught by the same instructor received the same assignments; they were not required, however, to hand them in. Thus their productions, if any, were not scrutinized; instead, at the next class meeting, questions about the problems were invited by the

11

instructor. Generally, as is so often the case, only two or three students had queries. On both the midterm and the final examination, which were constructed and graded by the coinstructor, there were no significant differences in performance between the two groups of students.

Lest readers from other subject matter areas dismiss those results as not generalizable because of their source, the results from a similar study (Sutton and Allen, 1964) need to be explained. Again, practice and feedback were manipulated —in this case in a course in English composition. A random sample of 112 students (47 males, 65 females) was drawn from a total of 394 entering freshmen; the sample students were assigned randomly to five class sections. Written compositions were collected and standardized tests were given during a two-week before period and again during a two-week after period. During the intervening ten-week period, the instruction varied from section to section.

Section V: At the first session each week, each student wrote a paper; during the second class session, the paper, having been corrected by the instructor, was reviewed; during the third class session, the paper was rewritten.

Section IV: Procedure was identical to that of Section V except that the paper was corrected by students enrolled in Section III.

Section III: Students wrote *no* themes during the ten-week period. At the first class session each week, each student read and judged papers written by the students in Section IV; during the second class session, each student reviewed a rewritten paper from Section IV; during the third meeting, each student reviewed a rewritten paper which he had corrected originally.

Section II: No themes were written during the ten-week period; all class time was devoted to the study of literature.

Section I: Students completed the after tests immediately following completion of the before tests at the very beginning of the semester.

All groups showed significant gains on objective tests —both the English Composition Test of the College Entrance Examination Board and the English Expression portion of the Cooperative English Test. There were no significant differences, however, among the magnitude of gains for the five different sections. Each student's before and after compositions were evaluated in several ways by five judges; no group exhibited any improvement in writing ability. (This investigation is one of the best in all the literature because of the very careful manner in which it was executed.)

Spending a specific amount of time in the classroom is another instructional practice perpetuated despite lack of evidence that it is sound. Although well intentioned, laws in Florida, Michigan, and Oregon (and similar laws contemplated in other states) requiring professors to spend a specified number of hours in the classroom each week—the magic phrase here is contact hours—may have the unfortunate results of continuing the surveillance role and encouraging professors to maintain the old teaching-learning stance. Such legislation is an additional counter to Gardner's proposal (1958): "It *is* important to accept the desirability of a rigorous reappraisal of present patterns and courageous experimentation with new patterns. This must include, . . . at the level of higher education, the trying out of approaches which place more responsibility upon the student for his own learning" (p. 25).

Illich (1971a) argues that, as a nation, we have learned to depend on school to such an extent we have concluded that the only valuable learning occurs there, and, consequently, responsibility for self has been transferred to an institution. Almost perfect documentation for this argument as well as evidence for the entrenchment of the surveillance role is found in another study conducted on our campus (as yet unreported). In response to complaints by students about their lack of freedom to make certain academic choices and about the interference of grades with "real" learning, approximately one hundred above-average, third-quarter, freshman calculus students—many of whom were aspiring to be engineers—were given the opportunity to choose among any one of three Ph.D. instructors, to change sections at any time desired and as many times as they liked, or not to attend class at all. Throughout the course, tests were not graded but were utilized solely for learning purposes; a departmental committee prepared the final examination and assigned end-of-course grades. On a questionnaire administered about three weeks after the course began, the majority of the students complained that they did not like the arrangement because they simply would not study unless forced to do so. On test days at least a third were absent. In two sections only four students, each on one occasion, asked that their papers be corrected—errors noted and so on. The results were similar in the other section in that almost no students completed homework assignments or requested that their work be reviewed. Almost half of the original one hundred withdrew long before the end of the term. The results of this study and the mechanical engineering one may not be contradictory, although students in the latter performed adequately.

The supposed necessity for small classes, even at the college level, must also be examined as evidence of the importance of the surveillance role—presumably, the smaller the class, the greater the learning. This belief in small class superiority is another ancient bit of faith; it originated around the middle of the third century, when a rabbi (Eurich, 1956) established the following rule: "Twenty-five students are to be enrolled in one class. If there are from twenty-five to forty, an assistant must be obtained. Above forty, two teachers are to be engaged" (p. 10). The rabbi could not have been issuing dicta

14

for college students or young adults; we have simply borrowed philosophies and practices appropriate for little folk.

Do advocates of small classes believe that their impact is as profound for an eighteen-year-old as it is for a six-year-old?

Current dedication to the small class notion is illustrated by the results of a survey (Hodgkinson, 1968) of some 1,250 faculty members on nineteen campuses via questionnaires and interviews. They gave first priority to "class size" among ten factors related to learning. Somewhat continuous reenforcement for the small class idea is provided by the persistent legend of Mark Hopkins on one end of a log interacting with a student on the other as the ideal arrangement for all learning. It should not be surprising that students, too, prefer small classes and give as their reason a desire for special attention. Yet, on innumerable occasions I have made arrangements to meet with them individually and then had almost no takers. Those very few who did visit asked simple nonacademic questions.

All the while, many small colleges claim superiority over large ones *because* of their small classes, their index of success being that *more* of their students than those from large institutions go on to graduate school. Although a pioneering study by Knapp and Goodrich (1952) corroborated their claim, when academic ability was controlled or held constant as a variable in several later studies (Holland, 1957; McConnell and Heist, 1959; Thistlethwaite, 1959), supporting evidence evaporated; intellectual ability was the factor, *not* the small classes.

Our limited and distorted conception of the role of the faculty member has been accompanied by an equally limited conception of the end product of learning—achievement. Pragmatically, it has been defined almost universally as scores on a test or series of tests. When converted to letter grades or symbols and averaged into an all-inclusive grade point average, these scores become the basis of all sorts of judgments about the student and his acquired abilities; it consequently exerts a profound influence in determining the direction of his life (see Chapter Three). There is even a trend now toward evaluating an instructor's effectiveness by an inspection of the symbols his students receive, a blatant denial of the complexity of the factors contributing to learning and a wearisome continuation of the notion that learning is something imparted by the instructor to the learner.

Now that accountability, although little understood, is the new panacea for higher education, one encounters all too often such dogma as: If the student hasn't learned, the teacher hasn't taught. The unvoiced assumption is that there is one student and one teacher and that both have nothing else to do. Also implied is a degree of control of the latter over the former which most Americans find intolerable and unacceptable. I am not suggesting that the other extreme attitude is correct: If a student hasn't learned, either he isn't very bright or he hasn't studied.

Official pronouncements of the colleges and universities however confirm that they do not view the learning process in the simplistic terms of their critics. Faculty members generally subscribe to the idea that learning requires developing a great variety of mental activities and qualities. They seem generally agreed that students should at the least learn facts, principles, and concepts; integrate knowledge from a variety of sources; develop certain skills, for example, written expression; apply or transfer facts, principles, and concepts to other situations; evaluate various forms of evidence or proofs; and become independent learners. Even though they may be insufficient, these abilities seem in no way to be incongruent with some of the current demands of both students and young faculty members for *relevance* and attention to the problems of society. Numerous questions may be raised about these abilities, but in the final analysis what is the evidence that students do, indeed, attain any or all of them, and if they do, why? (All the students I ever taught attained superlatively, at least during the first half of my teaching career!)

If the assertions about the prevalence of misperceptions and unsupported traditional influences are correct, what are the proper questions to ask about the promotion of learning? In the search for such questions, I have made a careful examination of research-based information, and that information is part of the substance of this book. My endeavor rests upon an abiding faith in the cognitive abilities of my some half million colleagues—if their attention can be caught. Faculty members are in *direct control* of many of the arrangements for learning; on many campuses, they not only control activities within their own classrooms but also determine to a large extent institutional academic policies and procedures. In the hope of provoking change in these areas, the remainder of the book reports teaching-learning endeavors which reflect an awareness of the changing nature of our society and the different constituencies with which higher education must now deal (Chapters Four and Five). Some of the new conditions for learning rest upon well-defined research evidence, and I turn to that evidence in the next chapter.

2

❦❧❦❧❦❧❦❧❦❧❦❧❦❧❦❧❦❧❦❧❦❧❦❧

Learning
Research and the
Locked System

❦❧❦❧❦❧❦❧❦❧❦❧❦❧❦❧❦❧❦❧❦❧❦❧

In the year of our Lord 1432, there arose a grievous quarrel among the brethren over the number of teeth in the mouth of a horse. For 13 days the disputation raged without ceasing. All the ancient books and chronicles were fetched out, and wonderful and pon-

derous erudition, such as was never before heard of in this region, was made manifest. At the beginning of the 14th day, a youthful friar of goodly bearing asked his learned superiors for permission to add a word, and straightaway, to the wonderment of the disputants, whose deep wisdom he sore vexed, he beseeched them to unbend in a manner coarse and unheard-of, and to look in the open mouth of a horse and find the answer to their questionings. At this, their dignity being grievously hurt, they waxed exceedingly wroth; and, joining in a mighty uproar, they flew upon him and smote him hip and thigh, and cast him out forthwith. For, said they, surely Satan hath tempted this bold neophyte to declare unholy and unheard-of ways of finding truth contrary to the teachings of the fathers. After many days of grievous strife, the dove of peace sat on the assembly, and they as one man, declaring the problem to be an everlasting mystery because of a grievous dearth of historical and theological evidence thereof, so ordered the same writ down.

Francis Bacon, the gentleman credited as the author of this little essay (Munn, 1962, p. 4), was being profoundly prophetic about higher education instruction of the twentieth century. Even the casual observer realizes that research has served this nation well in almost every field of endeavor and that many of the leading proponents of such scientific and scholarly inquiry reside within academe. Considering both the lengthy history and the vastness of the enterprise—between eight and nine million students currently—undergraduate instruction has been the recipient of an infinitesimal amount of systematic investigation, as succinctly put in the *First Report* of The Assembly on University Goals and Governance (1971): "Many in institutions of higher learning are prepared to scrutinize almost everything—the natural environment, government and industry, all manner of other institutions, foreign and domestic—but they are loath to scrutinize themselves and the institutions they inhabit" (p. 7).

This hesitancy to examine their own policies and practices does not mean that faculty members are unique or in a special class because a similar accusation could be made about members of almost all agencies, institutions, and organizations. The constituencies of the American Medical and Bar Associations, for example, continue to be loath to scrutinize their ways. The incredulous paradox in the case of higher education, however, is that the professoriate is the one group which expounds more than any other not only the virtues of but the absolute necessity for free and untrammeled inquiry into *all* domains.

Be that as it may, over the past half century, but mostly during the last fifteen to twenty years, a few studies have forced a wedge into the examination of some of the simplest aspects of undergraduate instruction. These investigations have covered a broad spectrum of arrangements for learning, primarily focusing upon the relationship between and among widely acclaimed and enduring approaches; for example, small classes and achievement. Achievement, by and large, has been assumed to mean the acquisition of subject matter content. Although most of the research must be criticized for its undue simplicity—there has been implied denial of the diversity of student abilities, interests, and goals; the aspirations of academic disciplines and professional programs; and the avowed purposes of colleges and universities—selected conclusions, for which the evidence is consistent and impressive, have now debouched. At the same time, for many facets of learning, research results may be equivocal if not nonexistent. Surely a careful synopsis of the major studies is essential to the search for the proper questions about future teaching-learning activities. In light of all the confusion, we must disabuse ourselves of certain cherished beliefs. My tactic in such a pretentious pursuit is that of mentioning a broad sample of the subject matter areas and of the conditions for learning which have received the research "eye" because faculty members have a proclivity for denying the applicability of research findings about learning to their own discipline, to their own behavior in the classroom, and in the creation of academic policies.

A novel investigation (Dubin and Taveggia, 1968) pooled the data from a large number of studies conducted between 1924 and 1965 on the relationship between achievement and instructional arrangements; in essence, the raw data from ninety-one studies were added together. This technique is in strong contrast to the usual method of adding together or summarizing conclusions from individual authors in an effort to reach a generalization; the technique is not ordinarily used in research on these types of problems. An uncritical pooling of isolated conclusions has the sometimes disastrous disadvantage of perpetuating the unsupported claims of the original reports. The area of instruction appears to have such an emotional aura for many faculty members and students that special safeguards are warranted; there is a tantalizing tendency to assign cause-effect relationships when, in fact, they simply do not exist. The institution of higher learning should be the last one of all to make unsubstantiated claims.

The ninety-one studies has examined, but were not limited to, the following courses and subject areas: accounting, algebra, American government, biology, chemistry, child development, education, engineering, English composition, history, mathematics, physiology, psychology, quadratic equations, general science, natural science, physical science, speech, and statistics. Combinations of comparisons had been made among the following instructional conditions: lecture, discussion, several arrangements of lecture-discussion meetings, supervised and unsupervised independent study, television, and programed materials (books and machines). Based on special analysis of the data, the authors conclude: "These data demonstrate clearly and unequivocally that there is no measurable difference among truly distinctive methods of college instruction when evaluated by student performance on final examinations" (p. 35).

This conclusion is consistent with several large-scale investigations not included in the pooling review. For example, in the Experiment on Independent Study (1958), conducted at Antioch College, different sections of history of Western art, instruction in the earth sciences, American government and politics, philosophy, physical science, and problems in anthropology were taught via lecture-discussion, small groups without the instructor, and independent study. Reductions in formal class time varied from 30 to 80 per cent. Before and after tests revealed gains for all groups in content understanding but no substantive differences between the sections of a particular course taught under different arrangements.

In another study, at the University of Colorado (Gruber and Weitman, 1962), time in class was reduced from three times per week to once per week in the following courses and areas: Psychology (educational, general); reinforced concrete design; freshman English; physical optics; man in the physical world; economics; marketing; chemical engineering; American government; analytical geometry; calculus; and advanced chemical engineering thermodynamics. Generally, content understanding, as measured in a variety of ways, was not affected adversely.

A most ambitious investigation (Macomber, 1957) undertaken at Miami University (Ohio) involved approximately 4,500 students and twenty-three separate courses: foundations of human behavior, psychology, air science, economics (four courses), business and government, introductory chemistry, teaching principles, composition and literature, essentials of geography, government, mathematics, physics, introductory psychology, social studies, introductory sociology, zoology, classics, elementary French (two courses), introduction to business, and introduction to geology. The study included three instructional procedures with numerous variations—television, lecture, and discussion—and classes of different sizes—small, medium, and large. With respect to acquisition of subject matter, there were essentially no differences among any of the groups for a particular course taught by the different methods.

As McKeachie (1970, p. 13), one of the leading advocates and practitioners of research in instruction, states in his review of the research, "So far as performance on course examinations is concerned, there is no strong basis for preferring one teaching method over another." To recapitulate briefly, most of the research in teaching-learning with young college men and women has tended to center upon single and easily manipulated surface conditions. Consistently, however, such variables as class size, frequency of class meetings, and manner of presentation, when considered in isolation, have been demonstrated to wield no major impact upon learning as measured by the usual tests. Even when some of these variables have been combined, their influence appears to be quite minimal. Because the variables are gross simplifications of an extraordinarily complex activity, however, it should not be surprising that there are no significant differences.

Nonetheless, because of the consistency of the results in different institutions of higher learning—for example, selective and nonselective ones—and the disciplines in and among them, a far-reaching conclusion, and one which undoubtedly is disturbing to many faculty members and students, can be drawn about the teaching of subject matter content: *If the content of a discipline can be defined as a body of information and concepts, the way or ways in which ideas or concepts are organized, and the methods by which knowledge is sought,* and *if it is acceded that class examinations measure content primarily—there being no research evidence to the contrary—then the explanations of such content by the instructor in the classroom, by whatever method, contribute little to the learning of* content. (This generalization may not apply to certain skill areas.)

In view of the plethora of paraphernalia (textbooks, audio and video tapes, slides, and so on) which present content and most of which are now readily and inexpensively available to students, the conclusion should not be startling. Perhaps scholarly perspecuity has been dulled by ignoring the all-too-obvious fact that textbooks or similar materials have been utilized by the students in all the studies. Furthermore, students have been conditioned over the years to "proper" patterns for learning and, given a textbook, a course outline, and an impending final examination, can covertly recreate the pattern to which they have become so accustomed: initial and continuing passivity with a final spurt of cramming. As a consequence, their untouched psyches nullify the effects of almost any externally imposed method or arrangements. Another possible explanation for "no significant differences" is mentioned in Chapter Three.

While there are frequent claims that most areas and courses promote critical thinking or reasoning, a spirit of scholarly inquiry, learning how to learn, and other non-discipline–bound abilities, few studies in the literature pursue the relationships between instruction and the development of those qualities. In the Antioch College study already mentioned, no relationship was found between any of the various teaching approaches and performance on a specially constructed Learning Resourcefulness Test; in the Miami University (Ohio) study, there were no differences among the groups on a Test of Critical Thinking. As for independence in learning, it was found in the University of Colorado investigation that seniors read about the same number of nonassigned books and studied about the same number of hours per week as did freshmen.

The research literature on changes in values and attitudes during college is voluminous, but many of the studies are difficult to interpret because of inherent problems in controls and measurement. Two important scholarly reviews of most of the substantive research, however, which cover different points in time, provide some valuable clues. During the mid-fifties, Jacob's *Changing Values in College* (1956) precipitated quite a storm in academic circles. The content was based upon an analysis of 350 studies conducted at many different institutions during the 1940s and early 1950s. The major overall effect of higher education upon attitudes and values seemed to be the promotion of a general acceptance of the standards characteristic of other college men and women. But the conclusion which provoked the storm indicated essentially no relationship between changes in values and curriculum or methods of instruction. The ultimate insult derived from the finding that faculty had little impact: "The teacher appears to have little standing with the mass of students and less influence. He goes with the books, the blackboards, and the audio-visual aids" (p. 79).

A conclusion which seems to have been overlooked by many was that certain small institutions did indeed make a difference in the values and attitudes of their students. The few influential institutions were those with a mission, and all members of the academic community—administrators, faculty, students, and other personnel—were dedicated to promoting it.

The second work was much more intensive and extensive than the first. *The Impact of College on Students* (Feldman and Newcomb, 1969) covered over 1,500 studies and was quite up to date. Overall, the values and attitudes of students described in the second review were quite different from those

25

of their predecessors. Over the four years of college, there was a gradual decline in authoritarianism, dogmatism, and prejudice; a declining conservatism about public issues; and a growing sensitivity to esthetic experiences. In contrast to the lack of curricular influence indicated in the first review, the second found that the curriculum (defined as the academic major) did have differential impacts on attitudes and values. The conclusion about faculty influence remained essentially unchanged over the fifteen-year period, and again the small-college impact was substantiated.

Meaningful interpretations of these two thousand studies are complicated by numerous factors: values and attitudes are nebulous; research designs have varied from poor to excellent; and little is known about the changes which occur in young people who do not attend college. A few studies (Trent and Medsker, 1968; Plant, 1962, 1965) suggest that the values and attitudes of nonattenders change in the same direction but to a lesser extent. Nevertheless, group influences—such as those of a small school or an academic department—rather than individual influences (faculty members) appear to produce changes in students.

Chickering (1969) brought together data from several studies which identify an additional group ingredient in or influence on student values. The data support his hypothesis that "when student-faculty interaction is frequent and friendly and when it occurs in diverse situations calling for varied roles, development of intellectual competence, sense of competence, autonomy, and purpose are fostered" (p. 153).

Little research has been devoted to such matters as retention and application of subject matter, although application is one of the major goals in most instruction (and by "application," I do not mean "training"). Such data as are available often tend to be equivocal, but one major study of retention and later application of subject matter provided some

26

highly provocative results (Kitzhaber, 1963). Themes prepared by freshmen at the end of their English course at Dartmouth College were compared with themes written by seniors in the great issues course (the seniors had taken the English course earlier). Careful sampling procedures and a meticulously objective scoring system were followed. Each paper was corrected for eight types of errors: focus and structure, material, paragraphs, sentences, words, grammar, punctuation and mechanics, and spelling. The seniors made from twice to ten times as many errors per category as did the freshmen. It is dangerous to generalize from this one study; it may serve, though, to highlight questions which need to be raised about many of our instructional arrangements. Most courses are not taught for the sole purpose of having students perform well only at the termination of the course; yet most instructional research has been the end-of-course type: It is easier to conduct than the long-range type!

Issues other than those for improving the instruction in a particular course need examination. In this regard, some of the research data about memory and that illusive phenomenon psychologists now call transfer of learning—historically referred to as formal discipline—may be instructive. The doctrine of formal discipline seems to be the basis of at least two of the enduring beliefs about instruction which were mentioned in Chapter One: information once learned is retained for later use in problem solving; and there is a direct relationship between knowledge and action.

TRANSFER OF LEARNING

Hundreds of years before science assumed its current empirical nature, it was postulated that the mind was composed of a set of faculties or powers, such as memory and reason, and that if these faculties were to develop properly, they had to be exercised, with "hard" subjects provoking the most

27

growth. Furthermore, a faculty so developed would then be utilized appropriately and more or less automatically or spontaneously when the need arose. Memorizing various materials during childhood, went the theory, would strengthen the memory faculty, and, as a consequence, learning in adulthood would be facilitated; the reasoning faculty if fortified by the study of mathematics, especially, would respond to nonmathematical problems in an appropriate fashion.

The foundations of formal discipline were laid prior to the coming of Christ and have been accepted uncritically by many scholars ever since. For example, Isocrates (Monroe, 1902, p. 107) remarked: "Schoolboys are trained to work and think accurately by grammar and literary study." Subsequently Plutarch (Monroe, 1902, p. 319) admonished: "The exercising of memory in the schools doth not only give the greatest assistance toward the attainment of learning but also to all actions of life." During the Middle Ages, John Locke declared (Fowler, 1890, p. 20): "Would you have a man reason well, you must use him to it betimes, exercise his mind in observing the connection of ideas and following them in train. Nothing does this better than mathematics, which therefore I think should be taught all those who have the time and opportunity, not so much to make them mathematicians as to make them reasonable creatures." A twentieth-century endorsement of the doctrine comes from Hutchins (1936, p. 84)—notorious for, among other things, some of his curricular innovations during the 1930s while the boy-wonder president of the University of Chicago: "Grammar disciplines the mind and develops the logical faculty. . . . It remains only to add a study which exemplifies reasoning in its clearest and most precise form. That study is, of course, mathematics. . . . Correctness in thinking may be more directly and impressively taught through mathematics than in any other way."

The two ideas central to formal discipline—exercise

28

and appropriate use of developed faculties—are now subsumed under transfer of learning. Attacks upon transfer of learning based on experimental evidence began early in this century and were prominent for twenty-five years. Presumably, the very first empirical investigation was conducted by the celebrated William James. Utilizing himself as a guinea pig, he tried to determine whether memorizing poetry would enhance his memorizing ability or faculty. He first learned 158 lines of Victor Hugo's *Satyr* and kept a careful record of the time required. Next he spent more than a month committing to memory John Milton's *Paradise Lost*. Finally, he memorized another 158 lines of *Satyr;* this required more time than did the first 158 lines. James concluded that all his practice on *Paradise Lost* had not improved his memory faculty. While, by today's standards, James's experimental design contained significant omissions, later rigorously controlled studies have not altered his major conclusion.

Bruner (1960) summarizes succinctly and clearly the present state of knowledge about remembering and forgetting:

> *Perhaps the most basic thing that can be said about human memory, after a century of intensive research, is that unless detail is placed into a structured pattern, it is rapidly forgotten. Detailed material is conserved in memory by the use of simplified ways of representing it. These simplified representations have what may be called a "regenerative" character. A good example of this regenerative property of long-term memory can be found in science. A scientist does not try to remember the distances traversed by falling bodies in different gravitational fields over different periods of time. What he carries in memory instead is a formula that permits him with varying degrees of accuracy to regenerate the details on which the more easily remembered formula is based. . . . Similarly, one does not remember exactly what Marlowe, the commentator in* Lord Jim, *said about the chief protagonist's plight but, rather*

simply, that he was the dispassionate onlooker, the man who tried to understand without judging what had led Lord Jim into the straits in which he found himself. . . . What learning general or fundamental principles does is to ensure that memory loss will not mean total loss, that what remains will permit us to reconstruct the details when needed [pp. 24–25].

As might be expected, experimental investigations have suggested that transfer of learning is not an either or situation, as past scholars alleged. Rather, learning is exceptionally complex, and whether a student applies or generalizes the content from a specific field—for example, mathematical reasoning—to other problem areas is by no means a simple matter. Transfer certainly does not occur automatically. Thus, old notions about memory and a direct link between knowledge and action have not been confirmed experimentally. The centuries-old doctrine of formal discipline has been shattered in the laboratory.

In the fall of 1970, a survey of almost six hundred randomly selected faculty members from six rather diverse campuses (Milton, 1971) revealed that startlingly high percentages of them apparently believe in the doctrine of formal discipline (see Table 1). It may be of particular importance that almost two-thirds of the respondents from the "hard" science area agreed with the second and third items, perhaps manifesting their vested interest in the educational tools being judged. And the fact that so many of the hard scientists believe in such a fundamental issue in the absence of the kinds of data they themselves would insist upon may be further, albeit presumptive, evidence against automatic transfer. One can only conjecture about the instruction delivered by these believers in their own classrooms and the bases for many of the academic policies which they help create. Many readers will quite properly criticize the three statements; only a few of the respondents did so.

Table 1. Percentage of Faculty, by Area, in Agreement with Transfer of Learning Theories

	Humanities N = 85	Social Sciences N = 105	Natural, Biological, Physical Sciences N = 183	Professional N = 221	Total N = 594
A certain amount of rote memorization of simple factual material (for example, historical data) provides good practice for the learning process.	47%	22%	49%	35%	39%
The study of mathematics is especially important in helping students learn to think logically.	26	32	62	40	43
One of the advantages in having students understand the scientific method is that they tend to apply the principles to everyday situations.	40	49	62	56	54

Alternatives to the Traditional

It could be, then, that thoroughly discounted notions about learning, in this case the doctrine of formal discipline, are continuing to obscure decision-making about undergraduate instruction. If, for example, we wish seniors to write as well or better than freshmen, other arrangements than the current ones seem to be in order; a similar assertion might be in order for other areas.

Are there other research discounted concepts of learning which continue to be prevalent in undergraduate instruction?

How useful is the coveted surveillance role in promoting non-content learning?

THE LOCK-STEP

Still another ingredient in undergraduate instruction which will bear scrutiny is the four-year academic regime. "Time spent" has been and continues to be an inviolable standard in acquiring the first degree; brilliant, knowledgeable, dedicated, and mature students lock step along with those who do not possess such qualities. Furthermore, for the most part, students are allowed to receive "credit" for learning by only one widely sanctioned method—that of taking courses. There is the great delusion, according to Commager (1960), that "everything must be taught, instead of learned" (p. 14).

Some evidence suggests that creative students, particularly, have difficulty within the confines of this lock-step. For example, at the Conference on Education for Creativity in the American Colleges (Cross, 1967), data from three highly regarded schools indicated that students who approach academic matters in ways characteristic of creative people are less likely to graduate than are other students. For instance, the Massachusetts Institute of Technology reported, that the school was "losing three times as many students who as freshmen preferred to try out new solutions, 'fool around' with ideas, or take

32

cognitive risks, as it was students preferring a well-ordered life with tangible results" (p. 2). Perhaps a reduction in time spent and a loosening of the lock-step are alternatives toward improved learning which can be implemented relatively painlessly. With that in mind, these notions are examined here in some detail.

Major concern about individual differences among students first began in 1921 with the pioneering work of Terman (1954); in that year he identified approximately one thousand youngsters with Intelligence Quotients of over 140. The group was studied intensively and extensively initially and again in follow-up field investigations over a period of at least thirty years. Pertinent to the issues at hand are these observations: 29 per cent of this gifted group graduated from high school before the age of $16\frac{1}{2}$; this accelerated group graduated from college $1\frac{1}{2}$ years earlier than did their nonaccelerated counterparts; a greater number of the early graduation group entered graduate school; and several indices suggest that the "accelerates" have been both productive and "well-adjusted" adults. Terman suggested in 1954 that schools were more opposed to acceleration at that time than they were when his investigations were in their early stages.

Interestingly, Learned and Wood (1938) predicted in the mid-thirties that "American higher education appears to be well on its way to another stage of development in which promotion will be based upon attainments. . . . Academic progress is to be governed by demonstrated achievement, rather than by conventional time standards" (p. xiii). This prediction resulted from their examination of the achievements of 26,000 students in Pennsylvania high schools and colleges. In brief, they found that many of the college graduates were no better informed on selected subjects than were large numbers of high school students. They insisted that an education must be self-achieved and that we must be "wary of factious aids that obscure the simplicity and arduousness of genuine achievement or that weaken a student's responsibility with overtutelage" (p. 44). (Approximately thirty-five years later, some attention is at last being given to the ideas these gentlemen advanced; see Chapter Four.)

Pressey (1965), now professor emeritus of Ohio State University and often called Mr. Acceleration because of his lifelong devotion to studying the promotion of learning, has also argued vigorously for decreasing the length of time spent in the entire formal educational process.

The most ambitious and carefully controlled acceleration project (Fund for the Advancement of Education, 1957) ever undertaken was the Program for Early Admission to College. It had as its purpose: "[determining] the wisdom and feasibility of allowing carefully selected students of high academic promise to break out of the educational 'lock step' and complete their schooling at their own best pace" (p. 1). From 1951 to 1954, 1,350 youngsters of superior ability were admitted to twelve institutions of higher learning prior to graduation from high school. Eighty-five per cent of the students were sixteen years of age or under, and 42 per cent had completed only ten years of formal education.

Evaluation of the project and of these young Scholars, as they were called, was about as meticulous and thorough as it could possibly have been. Unlike many other investigations, in which academic performance tends to be the sole concern, efforts were made also to assess both the social and emotional adjustment of the Scholars. These research endeavors were implemented by matching the Scholars with students of comparable high academic aptitude; the comparison students, though, had completed high school and were two years older than the Scholars. In general, the Scholars outperformed their classmates by a wide margin; and, year after year, a higher proportion of Scholars than comparison students ranked in the top tenth, fifth, and third of their classes.

Of special interest is the performance of three groups of Scholars on the area tests of the Graduate Record Examination at the conclusion of the sophomore year. Their scores were compared with those of the comparison students and two groups of first-year graduate students—672 studying at eight universities in 1955 and 1,201 enrolled in universities participating in the Early Admissions Program in 1956. The scores for each group of Scholars in each area—social science, humanities, natural science—surpassed the corresponding scores for the comparison students. In addition, all the scores for all three groups of sophomore Scholars were higher than those for the 1,800 first-year graduate students.

Although complete data about academic awards were not available at all the schools or for all four groups, the first two groups (1951 and 1952) of Scholar graduates received a disproportionate share of prizes and fellowships. The proportion of Scholars graduating with honors was higher than that for the comparison students; at the University of Wisconsin, for example, nearly two-thirds of the graduating Scholars received honors compared with about one-third of the comparison graduates.

Since the task of assessing emotional and social adjustment is exceptionally difficult, several types of data were gathered. It was found, first, that the Scholars participated in extracurricular affairs as fully as did other students; second, experienced faculty members rated the adjustment of approximately 90 per cent of both the Scholars and comparisons as being "excellent," "good," or "moderately good." Third, both the 1951 and 1952 groups were asked at the end of the senior year to respond to several questions (in essay form); the resulting testimony revealed that more of the Scholars had adjustment difficulties than did the comparisons. Many of these problems were due, however, to the fact that the schools tended to be quite overprotective in the early years of the program—in some instances the Scholars were isolated from the remainder of the student body. In addition, a large percentage of the boys had dating problems. Finally, a team of psychiatrists interviewed a sample of the Scholars and examined the records of all of them. This portion of the evaluation was deemed to be of special significance because it investigated the initial fear that early admission would subject the Scholars to excessive stress. The psychiatrists concluded, on the basis of several indices, that the Scholars experienced no more psychiatric difficulties than did the comparisons.

Approximately a decade after the original study, Pressey (1967) sought to determine how a sample of these young Scholars had fared since their college graduation. Since postcollege performance rather than end-of-course performance is the ultimate criterion, this follow-up study is of major importance. He examined the alumni records in three of the participating institutions—Oberlin College, the University of Louisville, and Fisk University—and sent questionnaires to the Scholars who had graduated from these schools.

Thirty-six Scholars graduated from Oberlin College; 64 per cent had earned an advance or professional degree, while only half of the comparisons had done so. These advanced degrees were obtained by the Scholars at a median age of 24.7 years (the median age for the comparisons was 26.6 years);—there were eleven Ph.D.s, eight M.D.s, two law degrees, and one degree each in divinity and dentistry. Eighty-one per cent of the male Scholars were married (the mere passage of time must have solved the earlier dating problem) in contrast to 72 per cent of the comparison men; 79 per cent of the female Scholars were married in contrast to 72 per cent of the comparison females. None of the early entrants felt any continuing handicap because of high school work skipped, and almost all felt they had completed their formal education "at about the right age." Only one male believed there was continuing social maladjustment as the result of early college entrance. Most of the respondents maintained that their experiences in the program had been maturing ones.

Because the alumni records of the other two schools were not so complete, the picture of their former students was not so comprehensive. Of the forty Scholars who graduated from the University of Louisville, 62 per cent had advanced degrees —seven M.D.s, six Ph.D.s, seven in law, one in dentistry, and four master's. Again, almost all who completed the questionnaire felt that their early college entrance had been stimulating and socially desirable—only two believed that skipping a high school year had affected them adversely or hampered their social adjustment. Of the sixty-four Scholars who graduated from Fisk University, 43 per cent had advanced degrees—six Ph.Ds, 5 M.D.s, one in law, and sixteen master's. The inquiry form was sent only to the forty-seven graduates of the last three years of the program for whom there were addresses; during the initial years of the program, much overprotectiveness had caused most of the Scholars to depart early. Of the twenty respondents, most believed that the program had been challenging and early entrance had promoted maturity.

Several institutions created early admission programs in the late 1950s and early 1960s and permitted students to enter upon completion of the eleventh grade. While accurate figures about the number of students who have attended college under this program are almost impossible to obtain on a nationwide basis, data from the University of Tennessee, Knoxville, lead me to conclude that the numbers have been very small. During the first year of the program, 1962, eleven students entered the Knoxville program, and the number has declined each year.

Other acceleration programs have developed recently,

however. At Florida Atlantic University (Stetson, 1971), for example, selected high school graduates may earn one year of academic credit through the College Level Examination Program (see Chapter Four). Of the 168 who entered between 1968 and 1970, 140 were still enrolled in May 1971. While the average GPA for all students is 2.57, it is 2.97 for students in the program for two years and 2.76 for those involved one year. Informal observations suggest that these students have not had social problems on this upper division campus even though the average age is twenty-three.

Still other acceleration efforts (Christ-Janer, 1972) include those of the University of Texas, in which all entering freshmen were offered the opportunity to take the American Government Test (one of the CLEP subject matter exams); approximately 70 per cent received credit. At the University of Utah, 1,278 students have saved one full year toward a degree by successful completion of CLEP examinations. The University of Maine administered the exams to the top half of the entering freshman class; 10,500 hours of credit were granted.

Perhaps the best known acceleration project has been the Advanced Placement Program. It was begun as an experimental endeavor in 1951 and has been sponsored on a regular basis by the College Entrance Examination Board (1967) since 1955. Able secondary school students study one or more college-level courses and then, depending on the results of rigorous examinations, may receive advanced placement, credit, or both when they enter college. The CEEB has conducted several major field investigations about the manner in which Advanced Placement students have fared in the colleges and universities. These are discussed here at some length because of the insight they provide about academic policies and faculty resistance to the "unusual."

Learning Research and the Locked System

In a mail survey (Casserly, 1965) of 763 colleges regarding their actions concerning possible enrollment of the candidates, there was great variability. Some students were awarded credit and placement even when they scored only 2 on the rating scale*; others were denied both credit and placement although they scored 4 and 5. In the case of 52 per cent of 23,145 candidates, the colleges did not award credit or placement even though well over half scored higher than 2.

An additional study (Casserly and others, 1965) attempted to determine some of the reasons for this great variability; sixty-three institutions, broadly representative of the 359 that received examination scores for five or more May 1963 Advanced Placement candidates, were visited. Interviews with college and departmental representatives revealed greater reluctance to award credit than to grant placement. (Awarding credit continues to be a problem with co-oping also and is of particular significance presently because of the surge of interest in experiential learning opportunities; see Chapter Four.) This reluctance was true primarily for a score of 3 despite the fact that this score is presumably equivalent to a college C. Noticeably prevalent were beliefs that a particular local introductory course was unique and unreproducible. In effect, many faculty members stated: "Advanced Placement is fine in other courses, but not in mine." This attitude was especially true in the sciences: "Our course is organized in such a way that if a student were allowed to skip it, there would be serious gaps in his preparation" (p. 17). The attitude was prevalent too in English literature. "Our (or my) approach to the course is

* All examinations are scored by a committee composed of both high school and college teachers on a five-point scale: 5—extremely well qualified; 4—well qualified; 3—qualified; 2—possibly qualified; 1—no recommendation.

completely different; no other course could possibly be equivalent" (pp. 17 and 24).

These faculty attitudes convey not only an offensive grandiosity, but also a limited conception of the dynamics of learning in young adults. (These grandiose attitudes surfaced in a study of instructional television; see Chapter Six.) If higher education is to be improved, faculty views must be broadened beyond narrow provincialism.

In another field study (Casserly, 1968), slightly over three hundred Advanced Placement seniors, selected at random, and approximately fifty Advanced Placement freshmen were interviewed at twenty institutions (including Brandeis, Duke, Columbia, and Williams, and the universities of Michigan and Washington). At ten of the twenty institutions, students reported not having learned whether their Advanced Placement work had been recognized until they spoke with their freshman advisors. (The CEEB goes to elaborate lengths to supply information to schools well in advance of fall registration.) Some college seniors learned first from the CEEB interviewer that credit had been granted four years earlier. Student complaints revealed that freshman advisors often did not know the Advanced Placement policy of the school; advisors were unaware of the nature of courses outside their own fields; advisors tended to push courses in their own departments— that is, insisting that Advanced Placement credit meant the student still had to take a designated course when, in fact, it was not required; and either "validating exams" during orientation or "validating courses" were sometimes required. Apparently, the possession of knowledge about local educational policies is not perceived by some faculty members as being a legitimate part of their role.

Approximately half the students interviewed had been placed in the regular college curriculum as though they had not participated in Advanced Placement courses. But a few students had been admitted with immediate sophomore standing; all of them were doing well academically and reported no problems as a result of skipping the freshman year.

I have examined the fate of these attempts to break the lock-step in some detail in the hope that a knowledge of recent history may be instructive in implementing recent and future programs. (Several medical schools—ordinarily bastions of caution—have integrated the four-year undergraduate and four-year medical programs into one six-year program: Albany Medical College, Boston University, Jefferson Medical College, Johns Hopkins University, Northwestern University, and the University of Missouri, Kansas City.)

Do studies about the lock-step and faculty adherence to it suggest that many faculty members have a very narrow conception of their role in promoting learning?

Should the classroom continue to be the primary unit for teaching-learning?

If so, what practices of the market place might be contributing to the maintenance of the rigid four-year system for all?

The Carnegie Commission on Higher Education (1971) recommends that the M.D. be awarded for three years of study following the B.A. and that "the length of time spent in undergraduate college education can be reduced roughly by one-fourth without sacrificing educational quality" (p. 1).

Will this recommendation be ignored, even in the face of the research evidence upon which it is based?

Finally, I would like to add that nothing in this chapter is to be construed as advocacy of lower standards. Unfortunately most proposed changes in instructional practices are met with that charge. And the research, I believe, suggests that

41

faculty have not much to lose by opening themselves to questions and continuing innovation. The research cited here suggests that the classroom and a given course are not the units which now need exclusive attention.

3

✕✕✕✕✕✕✕✕✕✕✕✕✕✕✕✕

Symbol Scramble

✕✕✕✕✕✕✕✕✕✕✕✕✕✕✕✕

One of the chief functions of an instructor is that of assessing a student's progress in learning. Such assessment can be accomplished in a variety of ways but by far the most common approach is the written test. The instructor prepares or constructs the examination which, if done properly, requires an inordinate amount of time, and following its completion by the student, corrects and scores it. Finally, in most cases, he assigns a letter grade or symbol; in many instances the A, B, C, D, or F is the only mark made on the paper. The student then has received what is euphemistically called "feedback." At the end of a term, the several letters are averaged into one and that one is recorded for posterity; thereafter numerous other averages are computed and recorded for posterity.

Any experienced faculty member will testify that the seeking of the symbol is more often than not the compelling force in the classroom and dominates the climate to such an extent that ideas and innovations are wholly secondary and often ineffective. Grades become the base of the learning pyramid and one cannot attempt innovations without giving it due consideration.

Grades and the attendant practices have attained an amazing prominence and status within institutions of higher learning—as well as throughout the nation—and numerous claims are made about their wonders; for example, scholars and scientists who are members of academe insist—often with passion and fervor and not with the intellectual detachment for which they are noted—that in working for grades students learn to think clearly and learn discipline, that competing for grades is preparation for the competition of later life, and that grades are good indicators of future nonacademic attainments. At the same time, many of their colleagues argue just as vehemently that grades impede real learning, their necessity interferes with the teacher-student relationship, and they motivate learning specifically rather than significantly.

Certain of these declarations are widely shared by the public, especially employers, and for any of them to be challenged with research evidence is indeed a rare phenomenon. It seems that the rationale for grading, more than any other facet of instruction, continues to be permeated by tradition, hunch, or dogma, and controlled by the hammer of academic freedom. Part of the problem in any thoughtful consideration of grades seems to be an almost unbridgeable confusion between the evaluation of learning—has the student learned those things he should have?—and the assignment of a symbol, the grade. The confusion is increased by an equally twisted conception of the primary purpose of colleges and universities as they exist for undergraduates.

Some have argued that much of the confusion and some of the malpractice in grading and evaluation are new, largely because of increasing numbers of students. In fact, in a delightfully enlightening paper by Cureton (1971), it becomes evident that much of the current unsubstantiated rhetoric is not new; it is merely another historical force which continues to permeate thinking about higher education. For example, in 1890 a Virginia institution had a six-point grading scale: optimus, melior, bonus, malus, pejor, and pessimus. Because, in the opinion of the president, too many mediocre students received the grade of optimus, the scale was changed to a three-point one: distinguished, approved, and disapproved. Shortly, however, the president again mourned, for "some bad scholars were approved, and good scholars were all distinguished." In 1905 James McKeen Cattell proposed that tuition fees be based upon grades; he suggested $100 to $120 for A's and $180 to $200 for F's. Incidentally, almost all who have expounded on this topic have claimed with dignity and great assurance that their utterances and proposals were either objective or scientific. Both those cloaks can be and have been used to cloud the issues.

Our perspectives about the essential functions of institutions of higher learning seem to have slipped grossly out of kilter. Colleges and universities supposedly have as their central mission the promotion of learning; fundamentally, and rightfully, grades should be for the purpose of assisting in that endeavor. A crucial element in the teaching-learning process is some means whereby both participants can know whether the

45

student has learned that which he is supposed to have learned. Can the student solve the equation? If not, what are his errors and why? This learning interchange can be accomplished in several ways, and it should provide direction for future teaching-learning. The assignment of a letter grade or percentage does not necessarily perform this service.

Grades or symbols are introduced into the process when, on occasion, it is desirable to convey information (expediently) about the student's state of achievement (or lack thereof) to additional parties—other teachers and parents—who might aid in the cause of learning. If the communication is to be effective (that is, to result in maximum benefit to the student), the symbols must have common reference points for those who interpret them, and they must be derived from sound and reasonable measuring instruments and devices. Any two or more measurements of anything, let alone student achievements, are directly comparable if, and only if, they have been derived from the same reliable instrument. It appears, however, that the order of emphasis has been reversed; that is, the *symbols* are now the primary concern of students, faculty members, and the public at large, while *learning* has been backed into a secondary corner, more or less a happenstance.

Warren (1971) documents this observation in an exhaustive and scholarly review of the grading literature: substantive issues have been avoided while there has been extensive fussing over pedantic record-keeping details. Upon categorizing two hundred articles and papers about grading which were prepared between 1965 and 1970, he found that about half of them dealt with the form of grades (a five-point or a two-point scale) and grades as predictive devices (if one goes back to about 1920, he can find literally *thousands* of these studies). The remaining half were scattered over a variety of aspects of the issue. Warren concludes that only a few statements can be made about grades with any degree of confidence: students approve of the pass-fail option but do not utilize it; graduate deans disapprove of pass-fail grading; and "undergraduate grades predict first-year graduate and professional school grades about as well as they have for years, which is not very well most of the time but occasionally quite well and occasionally not at all" (p. 4).

There is no need to document the great number of selection purposes which grades serve within institutions; all faculty members frequently hear some version of: "I'm going into finals with a 2.86; if I can pull an A in Poly Sci, I'll have a 2.89." (These numbers will be much more discriminating between levels of ability, that is, they will select better, when, with computers, they become 2.86125 and 2.89437!) Institutions of higher learning are also a vast certifying network for the nation as a whole—for industry, the military, and the professions. In this regard, Ericksen (1971, p. 3) asserts forthrightly: "Research provides absolutely no support for the rank order separations of 'merit' that proceed from second decimal point differences in the grade point averages of individual students."

Within this framework, what is the responsibility of faculty members—most of whom are dedicated to the promotion of learning—to examine the declarations and vigorously question current practices? Opposing this question with: "But what system can take the place of grades?" is premature until we are convinced of the need to extricate ourselves from the congealed cul-de-sac into which our energies are now directed.

RESEARCH EVIDENCE

Most of the declarations about the wonders and evils of grading are in the class of abiding faith; they have not received systematic investigation, and, for those which have, the results are not particularly comforting. Research into grading, of course, is plagued by theoretical, experimental, measurement, and statistical difficulties, and criterion problems are especially formidable. Such barriers, though, should not deter anyone from familiarizing himself with the research and learning what he can from it. Hoyt (1965) has reviewed forty-six studies, the first of which was conducted in 1917, on the relationship between college grade point averages (GPA) and achievement in several fields: business; teaching; engineering; scientific research; medicine; and others. In twenty-four of the studies, no relationship was found between GPAs and adult achievement; in nineteen of them, a slight relationship was demonstrated; in the remaining three, a high relationship was apparent.

One of the most comprehensive studies of the forty-six was that of ten thousand employees of the American Telephone and Telegraph Company conducted in the early 1960s. This study is cited frequently in support of the predictive value of the GPA; the criterion measure was salary. It was found that 45 per cent of the employees who graduated in the top third of their class earned salaries which were in the top third (ironically, it was found also that 25 per cent of the lowest third academically earned salaries in the top third).

The most refined investigation was of 426 Utah physicians: 102 full-time medical faculty members of the University of Utah; 109 board qualified specialists; 110 urban general practitioners; 105 rural small-town general practitioners. Over two hundred measures of actual on-the-job performance collected for each physician revealed that academic achievement (both undergraduate and medical school) was totally unrelated to measures of on-the-job performance.

On the basis of very careful evaluation of each of the forty-six studies, Hoyt concludes: "Present evidence strongly suggests that college grades bear little or no relationship to any measures of adult accomplishment" (p. i). To translate, if information only about grades is available to the prognosticator

the best prediction to be made is that the student who graduates with a C average or grade point average of 2.00 is just as
likely to perform well in postgraduate activities as is the student
with an A or 4.00. Miller (1966, p. 20), who reviewed much
of the literature about grading as an immediate aftermath of
Berkeley in 1964—unfair tests had been one complaint of the
students—reached at least one conclusion pertinent here: "It
seems reasonably clear that the grading system, at all levels
including the graduate one, tends to reward the conforming
plodder and to *penalize* the imaginative student who is likely
to make a significant contribution in nearly any field."

Possible long-term ill effects of grading are illustrated in
the results of an investigation conducted under the auspices of
the National Opinion Research Center (Davis, 1964). Approximately 1,700 graduating seniors from 135 colleges and universities were surveyed; all were National Merit Scholarship
holders, finalists, or semifinalists. It was found that the per
cent of such students receiving top grades ranged from 70 in
the lowest quality schools to 36 in the highest quality ones.
Many scholarship holders with less than a B+ average in the
high-ranking institutions however had chosen not to enter
graduate school; they did not feel intellectually capable of continuing the academic struggle. The fact that these young people were not going to graduate school is not the point. Their
self-confidence had been shattered. Was that necessary under
the guise of high standards?

The more immediate deleterious impacts of testing and
grading practices were demonstrated by Bowers' (1964) sampling of students in almost one hundred colleges and universities:

(1) At least half the students reported that they had
engaged in some form of academic dishonesty while
in college.
(2) The rate of cheating was twice as high for courses

with frequently scheduled tests as for courses with fewer tests.

(3) The rate of cheating increased when the instructor graded on a curve.

(4) Cheating was much more frequent on objective tests than on essay tests.

(5) Cheating occurred more often when the same test was given to more than one class and when the same test had been given in previous years.

(6) Although the majority of students who admitted to cheating were those with grades of C and below, over a third of those with B+'s and A's also admitted to cheating.

I do not mean to imply that testing and grading are the sole cause of academic dishonesty; it does appear, however, to be a contributing factor.

An almost totally ignored question about testing of students or the measurement of learning—both practically and theoretically—is one which has been of paramount importance to experimental scientists for many years: What effect does measuring have upon the object being measured? That question is really a paraphrase of what has been called the Heisenberg Uncertainty Principle; for example, when a neutron detector is placed in a reactor to measure the neutron population, some of the neutrons are absorbed by the detector with the result that the neutron population is decreased at that point and the measurement is false, to that extent. A homely illustration of the principle is seen when placing an ordinary thermometer into a cup of hot water. The temperature of the water is decreased by the temperature of the thermometer.

One published study was found (Meyer, 1935) which addressed itself to that question as it applied to students and learning. Slightly over 100 students were directed to study some material which was new to them. At the same time, each one was informed of the type of test to which he would be subjected: essay; true-false; multiple choice; or completion. Two types of data were collected and analyzed: subjective reports from the students about how they studied for each type of test; and the notes the students made and the booklets which contained the material to be learned. The subjective reports revealed that students attempted to obtain a general picture of the material for the essay exam and that they memorized details for the other three types of tests. The objective analysis indicated that a smaller percentage of students in the essay group used underlining and a greater percentage of them made summaries and maps than did those students in the other three groups.

The report of one of the students corroborates the data (p. 31):

> *For an essay-type test, I usually try to fix the general outline, the major drift of the subject, in my mind, and then add as many details to the general absorption as my time and energy permit. I usually outline the material on paper and try to think it through several times. When false and true, completion, or multiple-choice tests are expected, I concentrate my attention on learning details, definitions, words, figures. I stuff my memory with as many facts as I think it likely to retain for the required time, until and including the test, and then quickly forget everything except the few points that appealed to me as important.*

In another study conducted recently in England (Thomas and Augstein, 1970), sixty volunteer A students, twenty each from a grammar school, a technical college, and a public school, ranging in age from sixteen to eighteen, were divided into four groups of fifteen each. All students studied a paper entitled "The Genetic Code: III" by F. H. C. Crick (*Scientific American,* October 1966, *215*(4), 55–60). Immediately prior to the learning session, each group was informed about the type of test which would be administered upon completion of the task. Two groups studied with the impression that they were preparing for two objective tests; the other two groups thought they were preparing to produce written summaries of the material. In fact, all students took all of the tests.

All nineteen of the thirty students who produced an effective summary also scored effectively on the objective tests, but only seven of the students who scored adequately on the objective tests were able to produce adequate summaries. The objective tests were readministered to all of the subjects one week following the original study session. Those students who had acceptable scores originally on the summaries performed much better on this delayed test than did the other students.

A central part of this investigation was the utilization of an ingenious and simple "reading recorder." It was found, for example, that time spent in reading was merely a crude indicator of important characteristics of the reading process. Different types of reading strategies were identified. The authors propose that the reading strategy utilized was dependent, in part, upon the instructions about testing method. They maintain, however, that although material to be learned becomes increasingly difficult as the student progresses in school, the assumption that increasingly complex reading skills accrue simultaneously is not necessarily true. They hypothesize that low performance in college frequently can be equated with low skill in "reading-for-learning." It might also be conjectured that very few students have skill in "listening-for-learning." If these two notions are sound, it is no wonder there are "no significant differences" among such superficial variables as class size, type of presentation of material, and so on.

Should future research be directed toward understanding learning strategies of the learner? How possible might it be for young adults to learn new strategies?

It is interesting that the question of the effects of measurement has been so neglected. Again, we find a lack of application of knowledge from a given field—experimental science—to selected problems in learning. Psychologists (and social scientists, in general) who pride themselves as measurement specialists are certainly aware of the impacts of measurement and usually make allowances for it in their experiments under the rubric of the Hawthorne Effect.

One illustration of this principle was the experience with pass-fail grading for freshmen (Strong, 1967) at the California Institute of Technology. Beginning with the academic year 1964–1965, all freshman courses were graded on that basis. The impact upon the students was remarkable in that learning improved on a number of levels. For example, one instructor remarked, "They're reading books again." In each successive freshman class, however, improvement in learning diminished to a remarkable extent.

The criteria for testing and grading practices—that is, the standards by which an instructor determines the symbols he will assign—are genuinely puzzling. In a sample of four hundred schools (American College Testing Program, 1966), covering the range of institutions from those admitting all applicants to those admitting only the intellectual cream, grade distributions were found to be essentially identical from school to school. That is, approximately the same percentages of students received top grades in the nonselective schools as in the highly selective ones, independent of their respective ability and performance. Other studies indicate that as the ability level of the student body rises, the percentage of unsatisfactory grades tends to remain constant and, in some cases, to increase. Over a thirteen-year period, there was a significant increase (as measured by the Scholastic Aptitude Test) in the abilities of freshmen entering the University of California, Berkeley. The mean (average) SAT Verbal score increased from 487 to 550, and the mean (average) SAT mathematics score rose from 459 to 556. In spite of this marked increase in potential, the mean (average) GPA remained at 2.34 (Miller, 1966).

The distributions of grades from the 400 schools point firmly toward first the fact of grade curving and second toward the invisible norms which constitute the standards by which students are judged. Curving, with its attendant vacillating and sometimes mood-determined cut-off points, is the chief selection device; in many instances, this is for the sole purpose of screening or "selecting-out" students; that is, out of the institution, out of a discipline or field, or out of a course. The normal or bell-shaped distribution curve is a mathematical ideal or theoretical model; it is highly debatable whether or not any untampered test scores derived from students would form a "normal" distribution. There seems to be a widespread but erroneous belief that "mental" test data have been shown to form the bell-shaped curve (Lindquist, 1942), but the over-looked fallacy is that tests are deliberately constructed in many instances so as to yield such a curve. The rationale of the curve is violated thoroughly because the conditions which produce it are not met when any group of students, especially those at a prestige institution, are graded on that basis.

In a paper about grade distributions published as early as 1904 (Cureton, 1971) E. B. Sargent reported his studies on civil service tests and concluded that "there was a tendency among the best examiners to obtain results which gave the graphical form of a gendarme's hat." He thought that mathematicians would label this the "curve of errors." Sargent also insisted emphatically that careful grading could not com-pensate to any extent for poor questions—sound advice then and now.

It is amusing to hear psychologists, especially, discuss the merits of home-made multiple-choice tests. Such tests are "objective," they (we) say, because each question or item has only one correct answer. Thus no bias or favor can enter into

54

the scoring, which is often done by machine. All the "objective" scores for all the students in the class then are converted into a distribution, and at this point, quite arbitrarily and *subjectively,* cut-off points for the particular grade levels are selected.

The ludicrousness of much multiple-choice testing is illustrated by a portion of a paper entitled "If Dentists Dented Like Teachers Teach"; the author is anonymous: A dentist who is engaged in group practice—groups of patients, that is—is preparing a written test to be administered to his charges. He mentions this item to a colleague:

> *Does your lower left rear molar still hurt? (a) yes, (b) no, (c) only once in a while*

The colleague criticizes the test writer roundly because the difficulty index (a statistical technique guaranteed to aid in "proper" discriminating among students for the item) is too low and because answers would not result in a normal curve of distribution. After considerable debate, they construct this item, which has a high difficulty index—very few students will get the one correct answer:

> *What neural perceptions do you currently experience in the tooth which is anterior to and diametrically located with respect to your upper right front incisor? (a) Excessive neural impulses are still being received which can be interpreted as undesirable. (b) Neural stimulations arriving from this point are below the perceptibility threshold. (c) All of the above. (d) None of the above.*

The personal and arbitary nature of many grading practices and the potency of the curve is graphically illustrated by Dressel (1961):

> *In one university, the decision was made to section engineering students in calculus on the basis of previous grades. One professor, not knowing this, was assigned a group of students in integral calculus who had re-*

ceived A's in all preceding mathematics courses. Although recognizing that this was an unusually good group . . . on the first examination, he ended up with the usual distribution of grades from A to F. The reaction of the students forced him to reconsider. . . . The grades at the end of the term showed 40 per cent A's, 50 per cent B's, and 10 per cent C's. Knowing the caliber of the students, the professor still could not bring himself to report a distribution of grades in which almost every student would be given an A (p. 244).

Some nonacademicians are beginning to voice concern about the powerful pervasiveness of the normal curve of distribution. It was my good fortune to encounter *Peanuts* about the time this chapter was being brought to a close.

Linus: I have a theological question. When you die and go to Heaven, are you graded on a percentage or a curve?
Charlie Brown: On a curve, naturally.
Linus: How can you be so sure?
Charlie Brown: I'm always sure about things that are a matter of opinion.

The calculus study conducted on this campus (see Chapter One) illustrates dramatically one element of the symbol scramble tragedy—recall that very few students asked to have their papers corrected for errors or their learning evaluated in very meaningful ways. Since a grade was not to be assigned, they had no apparent interest in the learning activity. A similar study with similar results was repeated a year later with a different group of students. These few investigations into one essential facet of the instructor's role, marking practices, suggest that St. Augustine was indeed perceptive:

For so it is, O Lord, my God, I measure it;
But what it is that I measure I do not know.

Symbol Scramble

Elbow (1969), criticizing the ABCDF syndrome, proposes that professors defend it because "it expresses and means every nuance [they] intend." As Elbow points out, however, these expressions and nuances are the professors', not their audiences' (p. 228). In a mail survey of a few of my experienced colleagues, I proposed: "Imagine that an intelligent well-informed adult (not connected with higher education) asks you: 'Student X received a B in your course. What does that B mean?' How would you answer briefly?" Sixteen of twenty-two respondents gave simple straightforward replies. Each assigned a basic meaning to the grade—none equivocated; they were certain of their interpretations. Each one, no doubt, projected his own nuances.

Farther along in the questionnaire came this question: "Imagine that your son or daughter is in college (of course, he or she is a very intelligent, capable person). A final grade of C is received in a very important course. How do you interpret this grade to yourself; that is, what does it tell you about your child?" Now the replies took on an entirely different flavor. Only three of the twenty-two said the grade meant "average"; the remaining nineteen were uncertain, equivocated, or wanted more data. In effect, they responded as true scholars. One of them, who was especially cautious about the meaning of the C, stated he would be inclined to inquire about the competence of the "so-called" instructor.

THE HALLMARK

It is well known that educational credentials—diplomas, degrees, and grades—have served as primary selection devices in America for at least the past thirty years. It appears, too, that their importance has been exaggerated during the 1960's and into the 70's. Although there are many reasons for this state of affairs, one of the most important seems to be the

57

widely held belief that formal education produces better citizens, better workers, and better humans.

Richard (1971) traces the origin of these faiths to late in the nineteenth century when John Henry Cardinal Newman, Matthew Arnold, and others argued about the wonders produced in men by education. He quotes Newman, for example, as having written: "Hence it is that education is called 'liberal.' A habit of mind is formed which lasts through life, of which the attributes are freedom, equitableness, calmness, moderation, and wisdom; or what in a former discourse I have ventured to call a philosophical habit" (p. 5). Richard then asserts: "This charming idea has survived for nearly a hundred years now without a shred of evidence in its support" (p. 5). Nonetheless, current affirmation of the faith is found in these utterances of Hubert Humphrey (Barrett, 1971): "Higher education will solve the nation's ills. It will be the ultimate panacea for our troubled times. Therefore, we must move with dispatch to quarantee what will benefit us all." Once again, and in different contexts, belief in the doctrine of formal discipline has manifested itself.

Illich (1971b) labels contemporary education a consumer commodity and our preoccupation with it a pseudo-religion:

> *Today, faith in education animates a new world religion. The religious nature of education is barely perceived because belief in it is ecumenical. The dream that education can transform men to fit into a world created by man through the magic of the technocrat has become universal, unquestioned. Marxists and capitalists, the leaders of poor countries and of superpowers, rabbis, atheists, and priests share this belief. Their fundamental dogma is that a process called "education" can increase the value of a human being, that it results in the creation of human capital and will lead all men to a better life [p. 1464].*

Higher education, particularly, is caught up in an engulfing certifying enterprise—each institution of higher learning bestows its own seal of approval. Grades and grade point averages determine whether or not a student will receive the seal, and in turn, that seal is a mandatory key for opening doors which otherwise remain closed. Consequently, the symbol scramble must be examined from a broader perspective than just a few students in one classroom or on one campus— namely, it must be explored within the ethos of American society.

Berg (1970), in his book subtitled "The Great Training Robbery," cites numerous studies which suggest there is little relationship between formal education and on-the-job performance—a broader view of the (non) correlation between grades and later performance. He began to investigate such matters partially because he was informed by so many prominent officials in major industries about all the good qualities which accrued to young workers *because* they had been through four years of college; the officials also explained how the diploma was an invaluable device for screening out undesirables. These influential citizens were unable to document their claims about the diploma—they simply believed them to be true. Perhaps the most creditable and therefore sobering investigation cited was that concerning all air-traffic controllers who had attained Civil Service Grade 14 or above in 1968. Air-traffic controllers must have not only considerable technical knowledge but other personal qualities which higher education boasts it fosters—dependability, ability to think quickly, and so on. More than half of the 507 men in the study had no academic training beyond high school. By carefully analyzing exceptionally complete personnel records—useful performance records were a rarity in most organizations—Berg concluded: "Education proves not to be a factor in the daily performance of one

of the most demanding decision-making jobs in America"
(p. 173).

That generalization would be a bit more palatable and
meaningful if it were modified to read "formal" education.
The words "learning" and "education" tend to be used synony-
mously when, in fact, they are not. "Education" now tends to
mean a formal, structured, and often bureaucratic arrangement in which learning is supposed to occur; learning refers to
that internal process wherein an individual attempts to reduce
his ignorance. The air-traffic controllers had learned but not
under the auspices of formal education. Berg's conclusion,
nevertheless, is clearly an indictment of both higher education
and, when considered in conjunction with similar conclusions
from other studies, nationwide personnel practices which make
the possession of a degree a first condition of employment in
the absence of firm supporting evidence for the requirement.

Let me clarify my own position: I am not promoting
ignorance. Learning is good, in its most fundamental sense, because learning about the world, however accomplished, assists
all of us in coping with life. We seem, however, to be so
enamored of and ensnared by the structure of formal education
that both the process of learning and learning itself have been
forgotten. Rather than obliterating ignorance, we seem to be
submerging learning.

As for degree requirements, Califano (1969), who
toured the world in 1969 studying student unrest, states as a
result of his observations: "We must meet head-on the pattern
we are creating by making a four-year college degree the
necessary prerequisite for almost any kind of employment,
short of digging a ditch" (p. 80). He goes on to urge both
business and government (in its role as employer) to scrutinize
the thousands of jobs for which they now require a college
degree and to establish realistic qualifications.

A few voices are crying in the wilderness for separating

the roles of educator and certifier. Astin, for example, one of the most vocal, asserted in a recent (1971) address: "If the certifying function were taken out of the hands of the college, then the college could devote its primary effort to the educational development of the student. The certifying function has forced most colleges into practices which are in many ways inimical to their educational mission" (pp. 2–3). Jencks and Riesman (1968) also raise the question after mentioning the minimal effort made at Swarthmore College to separate education (or better yet, learning) and certification:

> In most colleges there is not even this degree of separation between education and certification. The two are inextricably and deliberately intertwined, each function being modified in some ways to facilitate the other. Certification requirements are constantly adjusted in order to ensure satisfactory socialization. The main consideration in setting many examinations, for example, is the necessity of passing students who have done the assigned work diligently, even if they have not mastered the fundamentals of the subject. . . . And no matter what considerations determine the questions on examinations or the relative weight given quizzes, papers, and exams, the most important thing learned in college may not be physics or history but the importance of credentials and the art of acquiring them [p. 83].

Ericksen (1971) concludes an exceptionally thoughtful paper entitled "Grading ≠ Evaluation" with this evaluation:

> Precisely because higher education has acquired a strong dependency on grades as academic currency, it will not quickly forsake them as a medium of exchange. And yet, communicating what a student has accomplished to agencies beyond the classroom is not a legitimate educational purpose and does not serve the instructional (that is, evaluative) needs of the student. The institution needs to forsake its role as quality con-

61

troller for society and to devise alternative means for managing students. Grading should not stand in the way of the more important function of the university: the education of a student, whether or not he can "make the grade" [p. 6].

DIRECTIONS

It certainly should be clear that institutions of higher learning cannot alter a situation so deeply ingrained not only in the educational system but society generally solely by tugging at their own bootstraps. There are some ameliorative steps, however, which can be taken within academe. First, tests or measuring instruments can be improved substantially. The measurement of learning frequently is conducted casually and cavalierly; test construction is time consuming and requires considerable technical expertise. Most faculty have had neither the time nor the training necessary for the preparation of adequate measurement devices.

In one of the very few investigations of instructional approaches in which significant differences were found (Gruber and Weitman, 1962), the results could be attributed largely to careful measurement of the experimental impact and the degree to which students had attained the objectives of the course. Students in an optics course at the University of Colorado were divided into two groups at the beginning of the first semester. Twenty-eight of them heard three lectures each week, received assignments to be completed outside of class, were asked questions in class, and took two one-hour tests during the semester—a conventional teaching approach in every respect. The other group of twenty-two students did not attend class after orientation during the first week. They were given a set of five major topics which were to be covered in the course but which were not identical with chapter headings in the text and thus were forced to search for appropriate material. Study groups of four or five students were formed. The final examination was designed to test performance at four points along a continuum of complexity of thought: simple facts and ideas on optics; application of simple facts and ideas to solve somewhat simple problems; difficult applications of facts and ideas; and exposure to and questioning on entirely new material. Four-part scores were calculated for each student. The conventional class out-performed the self-directed group on the first two parts of the final exam but the situation was reversed for the two complex portions. About half of the fifty students continued in the course—taught in the conventional fashion—the second semester. Near the middle of that term, a surprise exam was given, two parts of which corresponded to parts of the first semester final. The continuing students from the original conventional class continued to show superiority on "knowledge of simple facts and ideas" while the previously self-directed students showed superiority on "grasp of new material."

A second step is the abandonment of grade curving, which requires the adoption of a philosophy that veers away from discriminating among students for selection purposes and toward the concept of mastery. Indeed, pass-fail and pass–no record are movements in that direction. While the concept of mastery is a difficult one to implement in a college course because of the unclear limits of the material as well as other problems, it is not impossible. Mastery means that levels of performance are predetermined—and these can be along several dimensions, for example, a specified number of concepts—and the students either attain those levels or do not. Mastery means, too, that learning up to a certain level does not have to occur within a fixed time period of a semester or quarter. One teaching-learning arrangement which is in the direction of promoting mastery is P-I-P instruction (see Chapter Four).

Finally, distinctions can be made between those courses which require demonstration of some expertise and those which are for general enlightenment and personal satisfaction—record-keeping need not be the same for the two. Harris (1972), in an exceptionally thoughtful paper, suggests a way out of the dilemma of insisting that higher education is a private, individual matter and then demanding societal support for it as manpower development: degrees should be based on evaluated attainments rather than upon hours of exposure to instruction. Raimi (1967) argues that the present course system is the root issue in grading, and the abandonment of it the essential step in promoting genuine and substantial improvements in grading practices. He believes that if subject matter were organized into larger blocks there would be less fractionization of subject matter and a decrease in detailed tests. Both of these consequences would help to refocus higher education on learning.

One of the most intriguing proposals for the improvement of grading, however, is a multidimensional system rather than the present unidimensional one in which innumerable qualities or characteristics are combined in one grade (Elbow, 1969): "Grades can only wither away in importance when they cease to be ambiguous and magical. The present system too often allows the student to feel them as judgments based on hidden criteria, judgments which he cannot understand and has little power over. If he is rewarded, he feels he did the right thing but if the reward fails, he never knows which step in the rain dance he missed" (p. 220). Central to a multidimensional system is confrontation of a basic question: What constitutes good student performance? A catalog of components might include: command of course information; understanding of central concepts; application of central concepts; intuitive insight; verbal strategy; curiosity; and judgment, among others. Because different departments might place differing degrees of importance on the components, each department might agree on a different list. Any departmental list could be converted into a simple grid and mastery of each component judged as "weak," "average," or "strong" for each student. "In short, the system's flexibility would allow evaluation to be more closely functioned with the measuring instrument (the teacher and his course material) and the things measured (the individual student performance). *To the degree that evaluation departs from those two things, it is false and untrustworthy*" (p. 224, emphasis added). Research promise of the approach would be an opportunity to examine and explore the correlates of non-content learning.

As for contributions from the nonacademic world, I hereby challenge a large business or industry to recruit graduating seniors without any knowledge of their grades. Each recruiter would receive a statement from the institution testifying to the candidate's possession of a degree, and the recruiter would be free to obtain and record any other information he desired. The performance of these employees could be compared periodically against GPA's.

It is apparent by now that higher education is damaging its own professed ideals and, in collusion with government and business, is encumbering its students with a very contemporary set of hypocrisies regarding learning. In question here are grading practices and their effect on education, learning, and postgraduate success. In the next chapter, I explore attempts to answer some of the questions raised here.

4

Alternative Learning Schemes

One of the conflicts in which many institutions of higher learning seem to be embroiled at the moment is illustrated by this cogent observation: "Catalogue statements of colleges vary from the noble, elegantly put, to the impossible, patently stated" (McCann, 1969, p. 2). These assumptive catalogue claims, when coupled with the panacea pinnacle upon which higher education has been vaulted, tend to create

66

expectations which cannot be met; our colleges and universities have simply been setting goals too high for too many students.

The student population in the nation as a whole is already an exceptionally heterogeneous one (there is exceptional heterogeneity even on many individual campuses) and promises to become much more so than at present. The "elegantly put" and the "patently stated" must be tempered so that the broad differences in the abilities, interests, and goals of students as well as the diversity in the needs of society are recognized. Some students seek the simple, others the complex; some pursue the concrete, others the abstract; some are interested in the known, others the unknown. It is the rare student, indeed, who can master the spectrum, even though the conditions for learning may be ideal.

While I tried in the previous chapters to cling to research-based evidence, at least as a predominant theme, some of the material in this chapter must of necessity depart from that track. Just as I have made no pretense of surveying all the research literature about undergraduate instruction, I do not claim to describe all innovations. Rather, I discuss new programs which seem to be the most radical departures from our traditional teaching-learning activity—the surveillance in individual classrooms—and those which, when considered from very broad perspectives, especially from the perspective of the heterogeneity of students, seem to hold the most promise for the future. These new programs require substantial alterations in the roles of faculty members.

P-I-P INSTRUCTION

One of the problems at all levels of education is a proliferation of labels for complex techniques and procedures; the labels often obscure crucial factors and variables. In the case of personalized, individualized, and process (P-I-P) instruction, the labels may convey far more than is intended;

thus individualized and personalized may stimulate in many the vision of Mark Hopkins and one student. That vision is misleading and totally incorrect; in the Hopkins model, the onus for learning by the student is still upon the instructor.

The basic principles of the several variations of personalized-individualized-process instruction were first applied in the late 1950s in the form of programmed instruction (P.I.). The nation was over reacting to Sputnik at the time, and P.I. was among the panaceas devised to save elementary pupils from ignorance. Once again, however, higher education borrowed procedures designed for the very young, and college students found themselves going through very simple but very detailed programs and recording very simple written responses. One of the results was a consuming boredom. By the early 1960s, there was some recognition—as a result of experimentation—that although P.I. principles seemed to be applicable at all age levels, many of the mechanics of application needed to be adjusted to age differences. One of the fundamental principles of P.I. is that course content should be presented in very small logical steps. Studies demonstrated that the steps did not have to be so small for young adults and that the "logical order" of presentation was not always inherent in the subject matter. Time after time, for example, students would not follow directions (a frequent phenomenon in all instruction) and consequently would proceed through the material in almost no order, let alone a logical one; nevertheless, terminal tests indicated that they had learned.

Keller (1966) was one of the first researchers to do violence to conventional programmed learning. At the time, he and several of his colleagues were establishing a department of psychology at the University of Brasilia. Dissatisfied with conventional approaches to instruction and encountering numerous practical problems as they helped to develop a new university, these researchers ultimately resolved their conflicts by developing personalized instruction for a course in introductory psychology. Over the intervening ten-year period, it has been utilized in numerous fields and in numerous institutions, and by this time, as might be expected, variations in applying the principles of P-I-P instruction have been developed. The essential features, though, which distinguish it from conventional instructional efforts seem to be: the formulation of clear course objectives, also made clear to the students; the opportunity for each student to proceed at his own learning pace; the mastery of one unit of study—a unit might be roughly equivalent to a chapter, not to a "frame" or to half a book—before proceeding with the next; the use of lectures and demonstrations as vehicles for motivating students rather than as sources of critical information; the utilization of both undergraduate and graduate students as proctors—one proctor for ten students—which permits repeated testing followed by immediate scoring, almost unavoidable tutoring, and enhancement of the personal-social aspect of learning; and placing the *responsibility for learning on the student* (Keller, 1968). Born (1970) concurs with Keller that one consistent result is fewer low and more high grades than is typical; there is a shift from "normal" grade distribution toward a distribution reflecting mastery. There are significant differences between this arrangement and others in the learning of content.

One of the basic learning principles adhered to is that (in the technical jargon of the psychologist) responses which are reinforced positively tend to increase in frequency (or "nothing succeeds like success"). Every effort is made to create both learning arrangements and an atmosphere that students find conducive to learning; when they do learn, they are praised. Proponents of P-I-P instruction assiduously avoid the usual unpleasant, threatening, or aversive (one of their favorite words) learning conditions which are so prevalent throughout all of formal education and which so many instructors (and people, in general) seem to believe are absolutely necessary for promoting learning. One of the difficulties with negative approaches is that reactions to them tend to be much more unpredictable than reactions to positive ones. Furthermore, the negative approach seldom includes corrective steps which the student might take. Much is made of the fact that threat of failure and other types of punishment interfere with the promotion of many facets of learning, and there is great concern that the subject matter not be disliked (most of us, when given a choice, avoid the unpleasant). In this connection, Born emphasizes that student proctors should be selected not only on the basis of their scholastic ability but also on the basis of their patience and pleasant manner with their fellow students.

Fear of academic failure will be a major impediment for the "new" students of the near future, according to a report from the Center for Research and Development in Higher Education (Cross, 1971). The "new" students will be those who rank in the lowest third on tests of academic aptitude, and it is that group which constitutes the greatest reservoir of future attenders. Studies of this academically poor group have revealed an attitude of passivity toward learning and a lack of interest in intellectual pursuits. Although it is unclear "whether lack of success results in lack of interest or whether lack of interest causes school failure . . . by the time youngsters reach seventeen or eighteen years of age, it is reasonably certain that a self-defeating cycle of passivity and academic failure is well established" (p. 3). Positive conditions for learning will assume increasing importance if we expect this group of students to learn (or will they simply be selected out?). "It is high time to balance our preoccupation with how well prepared new students are . . . with some real concern about how well prepared we are for new students" (p. 3). A learning principle often discussed but seldom practiced is that of individual differences among students. These differences are perhaps most notable in the amount of time and energy required by students of differing degrees of ability and interest to attain comparable levels of learning. The almost universal arrangement of the same given period for all, a quarter or a semester, exists not only for administrative convenience but also to fulfill the selection function—"amount learned" varies within a rigid time period as demonstrated by the curve. With P-I-P instruction, each student may indeed proceed at his own pace to a level of mastery (obviously there must be some broad limits).

The personalized or individualized approach remained somewhat dormant until the late 1960s; by now it has been adopted in a variety of courses, including chemistry, mathematics, earth sciences, physics, engineering, management, philosophy, psychology, and statistics. The spectrum of schools in which these conditions for learning have been introduced covers the community college through such prestigious universities as the Massachusetts Institute of Technology. Reports by students who have studied under these arrangements are uniformly favorable. Such attitudes are in marked contrast to their dislike for large classes and active dislike for television instruction as has been shown in study after study, in course after course, and in school after school (McKeachie, 1970).

It seems entirely reasonable to infer that under such unpleasant conditions, students may also incur an aversion to the subject matter or content being offered. We may well ask what a student has gained if, with an A in history or political science or English literature or psychology or mathematics or any other field, he is thereafter turned off. Negative feelings are certainly not the sole result of the size of a class or of the impersonality of a classroom television picture, but the faculty can cope directly and expediently with such concrete factors. P-I-P instruction seems to be a major avenue for making needed changes in this direction.

The role of the instructor is altered from that of a

broadcaster to that of a manager, according to one of P-I-P's leading, but properly cautious, advocates, Ben A. Green, Jr., professor of physics and a member of the staff of the Education Research Center, Massachusetts Institute of Technology. Green (1971) emphasizes that the instructor will appreciate many aspects of P-I-P: he knows the class standing of each student; his course is defined on paper and can be revised readily; he can give individual attention to those students who need it; his students will respond to his careful planning; and his administration will be pleased that he can teach so many so pleasantly and at such low cost.

Lectures are not abolished entirely but serve different purposes which may vary from instructor to instructor. Green's variation (p. 7) is especially novel:

> *Lectures can be motivating, but they usually aren't. We do give lectures, but we make them motivating by keeping students out. We demand, for example, that a student pass Unit 5 before he is admitted to the second lecture (which may be in the fourth week of the course). The lecture is not supposed to be helpful (it would be immoral to keep students out of helpful lectures); it is supposed to be entertaining and interesting and off on a tangent. Students, will, in fact, work to earn the privilege of attending "enrichment activities," of which our lectures are the main kind.*

Several investigations have reported that attendance at lectures and demonstrations tends to be quite low (in most cases it is voluntary) regardless of the excellence of the performance; maybe other instructors are experiencing the psychic trauma which occurred to me a long time ago. Surely part of the motivation for nonattendance is nothing but youthful rebellion against authority; yet it may be far more than that. One of the most neglected factors in learning is that of attention. Each of us is familiar with his own short attention span and lapses of it even under optimal and highly stimulating conditions. Perhaps the students' nonattendance is additional evidence that listening to lectures is a poor route to learning. To reiterate, efficient teaching by the faculty does not necessarily promote sufficient learning by the students.

At least one institution is utilizing P-I-P instruction on a grand scale (it is called "self-paced" instruction)—Temple Buell College (Greenspoon, 1971). The school placed approximately half its courses on that basis at the beginning of the 1970–1971 academic year. Thus some of the experiences there and the lessons learned provide a broader perspective than that to be attained by an evaluation of the results of one experimental course. As already noted, one of the significant deficiencies of most instructional research is that it tends to be the end-of-course type, yet most courses are conducted in the hope of promoting lasting achievement.

At Temple Buell College freshmen have trouble in self-paced courses; their trouble seems to result from the fact that they have not learned in the past to manage their time. This finding should not be surprising because parents and teachers have been managing time for students for many years. But by the time the students are sophomores, the majority of them have learned to budget their time. Of particular significance is the observation of one faculty member who reported that her upper division courses were the best she had ever conducted when all of her students had been enrolled in self-paced courses the previous year. This report suggests that not only is content learned better under these arrangements but that the intangibles—interest, enthusiasm, and so on—are also acquired.

Questionnaire surveys of Temple Buell students reveal that dramatic changes have occurred in their relationships with the faculty. As more meaningful interaction occurs between members of the two groups, traditional roles become obsolete.

Alternatives to the Traditional

(In this regard, some faculty members have experienced difficulty with the change from a "fountainhead" role to that of a senior colleague.)

One group of investigators in biology (Kurtz, 1968) labeled such instruction the process approach and introduced an additional feature: By a variety of means, each student's basic achievement in science—for example, ability to perform simple arithmetic computations—is determined, and any inadequacies must be corrected before the student can proceed in the course. In one group of 144 students (80 per cent had completed a semester of college chemistry; 78 per cent had passed one semester each of college physics and modern mathematics), only 15 per cent, when supplied basic data about a cylinder, could determine the area of one of the ends and the volume. Only 26 per cent gave acceptable responses to the following questions:

> *The freezing point of water in degrees Celsius (Centigrade) is* ....°. *On the Fahrenheit scale, the freezing point of water is* ....°. *The boiling point of water on each of these temperature scales is* ....° *Celsius and* ....° *Fahrenheit.*

It is easy to see that many of these students would fail to achieve in biology not so much because of any inherently difficult material in the course but because they lacked the necessary mental tools. The data from this diagnostic testing raise numerous questions about promoting remembering and minimizing forgetting and seem to be consistent with those of the Dartmouth College English investigation.

Do these data suggest that the revered building block theory of knowledge has serious limitations, at least in some fields, and that adherence to it may be impeding rather than facilitating?

One of the most important elements in P-I-P instruction may be the peer instructors; several studies suggest that such is the case. In the late fifties, the Pyramid Project at Pennsylvania State University (Carpenter, 1959; Davage, 1959) demonstrated the appreciable degree to which advanced students can assist other students, and Webb and Grib (1967), experimenting with such diverse courses as psychological statistics and introduction to literature at St. Norbert College, give evidence that small student-led discussion groups particularly enhance the noncontent aspects of learning. Students assume more responsibility for their own learning and are less willing to accept stock answers, for example.

For several quarters on our own campus, Professor Frank Bell has designated ten to twelve superior students as assistant teachers from among the eighty-five to ninety enrolled in a junior agronomy course. He selects assistants on the basis of academic records, comments from other faculty members, and interviews with the candidates. Each assistant teacher specializes in a particular topic and helps students with their questions throughout the term and just before examinations; much of the tutoring is via telephone (Dial-A-Tutor). Course grades have been consistently higher since the program was introduced, and discussions with students, assistant teachers, and Professor Bell suggest that at least two factors are operating: the assistant teachers feel compelled to prepare thoroughly so they will not be embarrassed by their fellow students; and the regular students feel free to ask questions of and reveal their ignorance to their peers.

Why have faculty members so consistently ignored students as aides in the teaching-learning endeavor?

An instructional approach closely allied to those just discussed is the Audio-Tutorial one (Postlethwait, Novak, Murray, 1964). It is especially applicable to laboratory courses and differs in two respects from P-I-P: Opportunities are provided for the utilization of several senses in the learning process; and assistance is provided primarily by graduate students. The multifaceted methods approach is centered in a supervised self-instructional laboratory. Abandonment of the Mark Hopkins myth of one student and one teacher has meant that fewer laboratory facilities than usual can accommodate more students than is typical. The laboratory is open for many hours every day with instructional assistance always available. The student may come in at his own convenience and there is no necessity for him to see the same instructor week after week at the same hour each time. Advantages to the instructor include freeing him from spending so much time in presenting factual information and simple directions and an increased freedom to devote his time to inspiration, motivation, orientation, and meaningful personal contact.

The AT approach has been utilized at many different institutions in such courses as botany, biology, physical geography, earth science, and physics. Results are quite similar to those for P-I-P instruction: students' reactions are favorable, and performance is better than in courses conducted in the conventional manner. For example, in a course in physical geography at Western Michigan University (Erhart, undated) 20 per cent more students received A's with the AT approach, and over 85 per cent of the students preferred it over either large class conventional or television instruction. In a course in Western Civilization (Anderson, undated) at Montgomery College (Maryland), it was found that AT students were approximately 100 points beyond those in conventional classes. Here, although the initial student reaction tended to be lukewarm, it became more favorable over successive terms.

This approach and its variations, then, relieves the instructor from drumming deadly details into the student and enables him to become a student ally instead. These approaches, moreover, seem efficient vehicles for accommodating the heterogeneous hordes.

NONTRADITIONAL LEARNING

While off-campus, nontraditional, and experiential learning opportunities are not new there has been such a sudden and extensive interest in them that the Carnegie Corporation of New York, the College Entrance Examination Board, and the Educational Testing Service created a Commission on Non-Traditional Study in 1971.

In its initial deliberations the Commission (1971) found that: nontraditional approaches are being attempted more widely than its members had thought; there is great difficulty in precisely defining nontraditional education; some institutions are rushing into new programs with little preparation; a great body of mythology has already developed—experiential learning is being championed as both another panacea and a route to dilution of academic quality; there is considerable interest among students; and there is insufficient research. My own interpretation of the Commission's observations is that the bandwagon effect is already in operation and that the hunch portion of the "tradition, hunch, or dogma" formula for decision-making in higher education is operating rampantly.

Among the several conclusions in its first report, in view of the general state of disarray about nontraditional learning, the most important was "that much more data gathering and other forms of research are necessary and that these should be undertaken and completed as soon as possible if sound planning and programming are to result. Not enough is presently known about such basic matters as the types of student populations to be served, their needs, and their potential interest in furthering their education. Not enough is known about the suitability of the current examination process as a factor in measuring capability or achievement, to say nothing of new examination approaches that may need to be devised" (pp. 12–13). Simply put: "What will students learn in nontraditional approaches that they will not learn in traditional ones?" In my view, each institution that inroduces any form of experiential learning should do so on a research basis. On almost every campus, many knowledgeable individuals could assist toward that end. They should be consulted during initial planning stages because valuable data can be lost if its collection is not planned ahead of time. Almost all research about instructional programs is after the fact and thus deficient. Preprogram data about learning aid in understanding postprogram results. If each institution adopted this philosophy, the plea of the Commission would be met and future students might benefit in a relatively short period of time.

The increased popularity of experiential forms of learning is further attested to by the fact that one of the regional accrediting associations has already created standards for such programs (a frequent faculty excuse for not changing instruction is that accreditation would be jeopardized). Following a two-year study, the Southern Association of Colleges and Schools (Andrews, 1971), specified that there should be an adequate administrative organization, a sound financial base, a competent faculty, and sufficient and adequate facilities. There is no limitation on the portion of degree credits earned by nontraditional approaches; credit will be awarded via the continuing education unit in which one unit is defined as "ten contact hours of participation" in appropriately organized activities.

Experiential learning began in 1906 as "cooperative education." Engineering students at the University of Cincinnati were paired, and while one of a pair occupied space in the classroom, the other worked in industry; then the two switched positions. During the next few years (Auld, 1971), "co-oping" was adopted at such schools as the Universities of Pittsburgh and Detroit, the Massachusetts Institute of Technology, and in 1921, by Antioch College, the first liberal arts institution to participate. By 1950 (Wilson, 1971a), there were still only thirty-five colleges and universities with co-op programs, but by 1970 the number had spurted to 197. Whereas almost two-thirds of the 1950 programs were in engineering, these programs accounted for only one-third of the 1970 total. The greatest expansions, then, in recent years have been in business and liberal arts areas. Despite the recent spurt, however, less than 10 per cent of institutions of higher education include co-op programs.

The battle over the issue of academic credit to the co-op student continues. It has been estimated (Wilson, 1971b) that approximately 35 per cent of the institutions grant co-op credit as replacement of credits otherwise earned in the classroom. The remaining 65 per cent of the schools, however, either do not grant credit or increase the credit required for graduation. Again, if we had evidence of what students did or did not learn from co-oping such debates could be minimized.

Proponents of co-oping insist that a key feature of the plan is that work experience assists the student in bridging the gap between theory and practice—transfer of learning, if you will. That is, when the student has the opportunity to apply principles, concepts, and theories learned in the classroom to real and concrete situations, learning is enhanced and reinforced. A second argument in favor of co-oping has to do with human relations: students in the field deal with a far greater variety of personalities than they can on campus when associating mainly with their peers and thereby gain a more enlightened view of the world and its human forces. Tyler (1971) reasons in this regard, that work situations cannot be artificially devised in the classroom and that they do not arise from undirected relations with fellow students. He believes that co-op students do develop cooperative attitudes and, in a society where adolescence is prolonged, work experience promotes maturity.

Critics, on the other hand, maintain that the co-op plan: tends to distract the student from developing a sound foundation in theory; makes it easier for students to forget what they have learned when courses are interrupted by off-campus jobs (they apparently have not seen the data about "normal" student memory) ; and curtails personal development.

No doubt, both the claims and criticisms about co-oping will be advanced for other forms of experiential learning and in the absence of any evidence. Most likely the dogma portion of the tradition, hunch, or dogma formula will reign without hamper.

In July, 1958, a formal study (Wilson and Lyons, 1961) of cooperative education was launched; the research design encompassed collections of data from samples of students, graduates, faculty, and administrators from both cooperative programs and institutions without co-oping, and the collection of data from a sample of companies which employed co-op students. It was found that co-op students were similar to their non-co-op counterparts with respect to achievement in high school, academic potential as measured by scholastic aptitude tests, psychological needs as measured by a number of instruments, and rankings of selected aims of higher education. The one essential difference between the two groups was in backgrounds—a much larger percentage of co-op than non-co-op students came from the lower socio-economic strata.

A randomly selected sample of faculty members was asked to respond to a questionnaire. Sixty-eight per cent from engineering and 95 per cent from liberal arts either "strongly agreed" or "tended to agree" that they had evidence to support the claim that co-op students had many opportunities to see the relationships between concepts, principles, and theories, and tended to develop greater skills of application than non-co-op students. Seventy-five per cent of all respondents either "clearly disagreed" or "tended to disagree" with the criticism that so much time was needed for review when the co-op students returned to school that there was an overall academic loss. Using the views of the faculty (only samples of which have been given here) as expert testimony, it was concluded that the co-op program helps to give a sense of reality to student learning, contributes substantially to the students' ability to apply theory to concrete situations, and does not result in any academic loss.

Since it was not possible to administer tests to students directly, a sample of 2,250 students and a sample of almost 3,000 graduates from the classes of 1939, 1950, 1953, 1955, and 1958 (liberal arts, engineering, and business) were asked how they felt about the opportunities they had had to practice skills of application. For all groups a statistically significant greater proportion of co-op than non-co-op students believed their opportunities to learn to apply theory had been adequate. The Graduate Record Examinations had been administered to a sample of students in 1954, 1955, and 1958. The median scores for co-op liberal arts students on the social science, humanities, and natural science portions of the GRE were higher than those of non-co-op students and higher than the normative data for the tests. Co-op engineering students scored higher on the advanced engineering test of the GRE than did a standardizing group.

While the samples were small, and thus suggest a cautious interpretation, the results hardly point toward academic suffering by co-op students; indeed, they point toward academic enhancement. But other recent studies corroborate this finding. Baker (1969) found that when co-op/non-co-op students were matched on the basis of academic ability, the former out-achieved the latter as measured by GPA's. In a similar study (Lindenmeyer, 1967) involving 180 co-ops and

58 non-co-ops who were neither different in ability nor in achievement as determined during their first six quarters in residence, it was found that co-op students performed better than did the non-co-op students during subsequent periods on the campus and that a greater percentage of the former graduated in engineering.

As the basis of another study (Rodes, 1968), questionnaires were sent to 1,011 co-op degree graduates of the General Motors Institute, all of whom were employees of General Motors Corporation; the graduating classes of 1966, 1961, 1956, and 1951 were sampled. Seventy-five percent of 763 recipients responded. Questionnaires also went to supervisors; of the 179 who replied, 43 of them were co-op graduates themselves. Eighty-six percent of the graduates and 70 per cent of the supervisors believed that co-op students made a better transition into industry. About three-fourths of each group of respondents indicated that the co-op students had a much better grasp of engineering knowledge and practices upon entry into full-time employment. In the remainder of the questions, the perceived differences between co-op and non-co-op students were blurred. This was true for such abilities as: "demonstrating initiative and resourcefulness"; "supervising others"; "supporting organizational goals"; "participating in outside activities"; and so on.

Although research evidence about co-oping, the oldest of the nontraditional approaches to learning, is sparse, it suggests that many claims relating co-oping to enhanced learning are indeed correct. With far better research facilities available now than in 1958, when the only major investigation was launched, additional data should be sought for all types of nontraditional learning.

The University Without Walls (Baskin, 1970) is another nontraditional approach which is based on the rationale that piecemeal reforms can be temporarily palliative but not redemptive. Drawing upon two contemporary aspects of education—the diverse student population and unexplored learning resources—the fundamental purpose of the University Without Walls is to produce life-long learners, not graduates. Approximately twenty well-established institutions of higher learning are now participating in the program: Antioch, Goddard, and Chicago State colleges, the universities of Massachusetts, Minnesota, and South Carolina; Shaw University; and Staten Island Community College are among them. While the particulars vary from school to school, the basic organizational concepts for each University Without Walls unit include: participation by students, faculty members, and administrators in the design and development of the program; the utilization of flexible time units and curriculum—both will be tailored to each student; the employment of a broad array of opportunities for learning, both on- and off-campus; the inclusion of an adjunct faculty composed of capable people from many fields but whose life work has not been academic; and the utilization of existing community facilities rather than the construction of new buildings.

Programs were begun in the fall of 1971 with pilot groups of between thirty-five and fifty-five students; the largest group was 130 (Baskin, 1972). Some 250 persons, many of them having attained prominence in their respective fields, are serving as adjuncts. The role of regular faculty members is principally that of advising and planning rather than regular classroom instruction.

Another concentrated and systematic effort to promote experiential learning within the framework of traditional degree programs is the Living Learning Center at the University of Minnesota (Walz, 1971)—not to be confused with residential arrangements under similar names—which was established in September, 1969. Therein a student, working with a faculty member, plans very carefully how he will pursue a particular

83

problem, how his performance will be evaluated, and the number of credit hours which will be awarded. The program is open to all undergraduate students, and a student may study almost anywhere in the world. This program seems especially appealing because it is under the control of the faculty, and the student is required to plan carefully before a project is undertaken. Furthermore, specific evaluation of the work is included.

Implementation of its major goal of providing experiential learning opportunities was augmented by the creation of the Inter-Cultural Specialist Program and by the Teacher Service Corps. In the former, individuals from the community help with formal classes and innovative programs of the university. The Teacher Service Corps is comprised of recent baccalaureate graduates who assist students in designing and executing their projects. During its two academic years of operation, slightly over five thousand students availed themselves of experiential learning opportunities through the Center.

The new Empire State College (1971) in New York is a nonresidential school founded in 1971. It is anticipated that by 1973 it will include ten thousand students studying at a network of regional learning centers; the coordinating center is located in Saratoga Springs. "The main task of Empire State College is to provide resources which help students clarify and enlarge their own purposes and pursue the increased competence and awareness those purposes require. Since learning occurs in many diverse situations, the resources required are not limited to a classroom or campus; they include diverse persons and experiences in varying places, reached through multiple approaches" (*Bulletin,* p. 31).

Students will pursue most of their college education without residing physically on a campus or meeting in a classroom; there will be some opportunities for both, but most of the academic program will be pursued elsewhere. Application and admission of students will go on continuously throughout the academic year. Students will include young people who will take major responsibility for their programs of study; older people who have special interests; employed adults; retired people pursuing new careers, and, in fact, adults of any age who are interested in learning.

Learning is conceptualized as occurring through three basic modes: discipline, problem, and experience. In the discipline mode, the student pursues the usual specialized bodies of knowledge; this is accomplished by enrollment in courses at a nearby institution or by the utilization of books and other appropriate materials. In the problem mode, the student focuses upon a major problem or issue which requires knowledge, methods, and skills from several sources. The experience mode is essentially experiential learning opportunities. Flexibility is the key to all of the modes.

The central guiding concept about learning and the technique of implementation is the contract. Shortly after admission, each student and a mentor (a faculty member) co-operatively create a contract which spells out in detail a program the student will pursue, how it will be pursued, and how his accomplishments will be judged. The contract also specifies the responsibilities of the mentor. Contracts early in the student's career may be completed in a short period of time—for example, one month. But all contracts are very detailed. If reading is required, the particular books are listed, deadlines for completion of work are stated, and the exact methods by which evaluation will be conducted are indicated—tests, papers, reports from supervisors, and so on.

Minnesota Metropolitan State College, an upper division institution, opened in February, 1972, with one hundred students (Sweet, 1972). It does not have centralized facilities, is designed for those above college age (75 per cent of the students will be over twenty-five), extensively utilizes community rather than regular faculty members (a ratio of 10 to 1 is planned), makes the student the principal architect of his education—because the student must bear the consequences—and will measure competence rather than counting credit hours. Currently, it is anticipated that students will demonstrate competence in four areas (which do not lend themselves to neat labels): projecting and receiving communications; being a self-governing individual; functioning in the market-place; and coping with life.

The Bachelor of Liberal Studies degree program was launched at the University of Oklahoma in 1961 (Troutt, 1971). It is designed for adults who present either a high school diploma or its equivalent and is developed around the theme, "Man in the Twentieth Century." There is heavy reliance upon guided independent study and intensive residential seminars of only three or four weeks' duration. The student enrolls in one of three areas—humanities, social sciences, and natural sciences—rather than in separate courses. His work may be pursued at whatever pace he desires. During the first ten years of the program, BLS degrees were conferred upon 249 candidates. Withdrawals have been close to 39 per cent (for regular students, the withdrawal rate is 47 per cent). On the GRE area tests, 77 per cent scored above the mean in the social sciences, 70 per cent above the mean in the humanities, and 79 per cent above the mean in natural sciences.

Relying heavily upon independent study and modern communications, the Open University in Great Britain, is departing from the traditional residential/classroom sole route to learning on a grand scale (Eurich and Schwenkmeyer, 1971). With an initial enrollment of 25,000 and a budget approximating fifteen million dollars, the Open University blends television, radio, and correspondence instruction and 220 local study centers. There are no formal entrance requirements; anyone twenty-one or over who resides in Great Britian may enroll. Four foundation courses were offered initially (second, third, and fourth-level courses are being planned) in mathematics, science, social sciences, and humanities. Each course consists of thirty-six units of work presented weekly via radio, television, and correspondence. The local study centers are staffed by counselors, who assist the students in planning their programs, and by class tutors, who are local experts in each foundation course. They offer regularly scheduled seminars which amplify the material presented on radio, television, and in correspondence texts. Centers are equipped with radio and television facilities so that students who missed a program or do not have such facilities at home may receive play-back. Great efforts have been made to create lively and dynamic television programs.

As already emphasized by the Commission on Non-Traditional Study, evaluation of experiential learning continues to be a problem primarily because few tools and devices are available. The College Entrance Examination Board, however, has created several standardized tests which have been utilized in several institutions but continually encounter faculty resistance. Jencks and Riesman (1968) offer some insight as to why: "Such tests reward able but indolent students and penalize the inept but diligent. They thus undermine teachers' and school administrators' hold over their students. By emphasizing the luck of the genetic draw, the tests also puncture the myth that the young can expect to achieve success as adults simply by working hard and doing what they are told. . . . The use of 'impersonal' national tests, on the other hand, frees the young from the control of those adults they see day by day, and makes the future depend more on the students' intrinsic qualities" (pp. 63–64).

Nevertheless, the College Level Examination Program (CLEP) (College Entrance Examination Board, 1970) offers a variety of measuring instruments, all of which have been constructed by several academic and psychometric authorities;

each test "stresses understanding, the ability to perceive relationships, and a grasp of basic principles and concepts. It is assumed, however, that implicit in the mastery of any field is a command of certain basic facts. The examinations are carefully standardized nationally on college students who have completed the appropriate course" (p. 23). One of the fundamental assumptions upon which the tests are based is that "institutions of higher education must be concerned primarily with what an individual knows, not how many hours he has sat in class or the number of credits he has amassed" (pp. 7–8).

The CLEP general examinations are designed to measure what an individual student generally learns during the first two years of undergraduate study. The subject examinations are quite specific, however, and approximately thirty of them are now available. During the academic year 1971–72, around 150,000 persons will have taken CLEP examinations for possible credit in one thousand colleges and universities (Jacobson, 1972). These examinations, which have been constructed with such great care, are certainly major research tools for evaluating all forms of learning—both traditional and nontraditional. They are also being pressed into service for accelerating young students (as noted in Chapter Two) and assisting those older than the college-age norm of eighteen to twenty-two in pursuing their learning (this is consistent with one of the recommendations of the Commission on Non-Traditional Study).

The University of Missouri at St. Louis, for example, has created the Circuit Rider Program (Fagin, 1971) through which adults receive college credit via both CLEP general and subject examinations. Of 875 individuals who took the former, slightly over half had acceptable scores on at least one subtest. Of 98 persons who took the latter, 37, or 38 per cent, had acceptable scores. The Circuit participants represented a wide range of educational backgrounds, socio-economic levels, and employment experience; ages ranged from seventeen to seventy-five years and the great majority were over twenty.

PLEASE DO NOT FOLD, SPINDLE, OR MUTILATE

These programs represent significant beginning departures from a number of hallowed routes to and sacred ingredients for instruction. The surveillance role of the faculty is diminished; responsibility for learning is upon the student; rigidity is giving way to flexibility; there is a switch from a narrow view of how a student learns to what he learns; and, finally, a college education is no longer viewed as the prerogative solely of the pampered late adolescent—it is also for those citizens who helped make it all possible in the first place.

5

⊱⊰⊱⊰⊱⊰⊱⊰⊱⊰⊱⊰⊱⊰⊱⊰⊱⊰⊱⊰⊱⊰

Interdisciplinary Approach

⊱⊰⊱⊰⊱⊰⊱⊰⊱⊰⊱⊰⊱⊰⊱⊰⊱⊰⊱⊰⊱⊰

One of the oft-stated goals of higher education is the integration of knowledge from several disciplines. Judging by the manner in which knowledge has been divided into departmental domains and even further into a plethora of rather discrete courses, however, it seems evident that the goal has not been realized except by a very few exceptionally capable students.

Interdisciplinary Approach

During the past few years, and especially with the advent of the ecology movement, serious efforts have been made in the direction of correcting higher education's deficiencies along these lines. Numerous small colleges, in particular, have instituted interdisciplinary courses as vehicles for doing so; a theme is chosen, such as "Science and Man," and several specialists then present the ways in which their disciplines view the issues. While there is virtually no careful documentation about the success of such efforts, they seem to rest upon one or two interesting and dubitable assumptions: narrowly trained specialists have already integrated knowledge from a variety of fields or disciplines; these specialists, who tend to lead autonomous and isolated academic lives, can get together and more or less spontaneously begin to demonstrate to students how their various disciplines fit together.

STRUCTURAL ARRANGEMENTS

The new Evergreen State College, however, has chosen not to operate its interdisciplinary program on the basis of either of those assumptions. Located in Olympia, Washington, it is the first tax supported four-year college to be founded by the state legislature since the turn of the century. Its organizational structure forces faculty members from diverse disciplines to work together toward dealing with common academic problems over a long period of time. This, of course, is a drastic departure from the traditional faculty role, one professor/ one course/one classroom, which most of us are thoroughly indoctrinated into.

In their Coordinated Studies, as the interdisciplinary program is called, approximately one hundred students and five faculty members work together for periods as long as one year on such demanding topics as Causality, Freedom, and Chance; Contemporary American Minorities; the Individual, the Citizen, and the State; and Space, Time, and Form. In some of the Coordinated Studies, a student may earn a full year's academic credit by participating only in that program. The student is expected to spend up to thirty-two hours with the faculty members in a typical work week and there are numerous routes to learning: films, discussions, lectures, reading, field trips, special research, and so on. But the demands upon the student are coherent, not conflicting, as is the usual case in which a student must drop and pick up pieces of work in four or five unrelated subjects every other day. In view of the questions raised about grading in Chapter Three, it is noteworthy to mention here that students at Evergreen will not be judged exclusively by tests or other conventional standards. In essence, the official description indicates that "one of the most important advantages of the small and intimate community within a program is that continual and careful evaluation of each student's work becomes possible" (Evergreen State College, *Bulletin,* 1971).

As for faculty workload, each one participating in a Coordinated Studies program carries a credit-defined load of 300 quarter hours (Shoben, 1971). This might be contrasted with a conventional situation in which a faculty member with one quarter-system course enrolling 100 students, each of whom receives three hours credit, would generate 300 quarter hours. This certainly appears to be a reasonable workload, from the standpoint of both the individual faculty member and institutional cost. It is to be hoped that the entire program will be followed very carefully. Meanwhile, certain poignant questions seem to leap from these observations about notably laudable efforts:

With what success can faculty members be expected to execute an about-face in their instructional role?

With what success can an appreciable number of students be expected to chance the change within a certifying system?

Another institution which has departed from the traditional teaching-learning structure is the University of Wisconsin at Green Bay. Chancellor Edward W. Weidner said, in his address to the faculty when the school opened in 1969:

We must give up the comfortable old idea that professors meet their classes and post office hours (two or three hours a week) and then hide the rest of the week. . . . Of course you must have formal office hours. But we are at the time now when we should be available the clock around. If a month goes past and you have not had any students in your home, then there is something wrong with your approach to students. And if a week goes past and you have not had coffee with some students, if you have not got lost in some of our new people pockets, then there is something wrong. . . . If any of us are uncomfortable with students outside the classroom, then we ought to find another job, because the time is gone when higher education is a thing that takes place in the classroom [Fischer, 1971, p. 26].

Indeed, the curriculum is so structured that a faculty member cannot remain isolated from other people and from ideas in other disciplines. The central concept here is man and his environment. The school takes the position that every field of study and every profession has a social responsibility as well as technical expertise but that too many universities emphasize the latter and ignore the former. In implementing their transdisciplinary and interdisciplinary approach, academic departments—faltering faculty fiefdoms—have been avoided, and, as a consequence, faculty roles have changed.

There are four theme colleges—The College of Creative Communication, The College of Community Sciences, The College of Environmental Sciences, and The College of Human Biology—plus a School of Professional Studies, and within each college there are several Concentrations. A Con-

93

centration is really a kind of major in that the student pursues a particular environmental theme in depth and does so across college and disciplinary lines. The Concentrations include: Communication-Action, Ecosystems Analysis, Environmental Control, Human Adaptability, Modernization Processes, Population Dynamics, and Urban Analysis. Each Concentration encompasses several academic disciplines but knowledge from each one is focused upon the problem at hand and integrated with knowledge from other disciplines. The primary vehicle for the pursuit of learning as far as students are concerned is flexibility. University requirements are few but include a liberal education seminar, which must be taken each year, and demonstrated proficiency in certain tool subjects such as mathematics. A Concentration must have been selected by the junior year, but there are no rigid routes to it, and each student may choose a variety of approaches. Two additionally distinctive and novel practices are in operation: members of the community participate in both the creation and implementation of academic programs; and students are reminded that the initiative for any assistance they might need is theirs, not the faculty's.

Sufficient time has not elapsed for any extensive evaluations, but judging by informal reports (Hartley, 1972a) the goal of faculty contact with students is being realized. Formal teaching loads are not light, there are heavy committee responsibilities, and faculty members spend an "infinity of hours with students." In addition, a sample of 1970–71 students responded as follows (Hartley, 1972b) to selected questions on a Course Comments Questionnaire:

(1) "I became aware of ways the subject is involved in my own life." On a scale from 1 to 5, 3.5 per cent checked 1 (not at all); 7.7 per cent 2; 21.5 per cent 3; 31.2 per cent 4; and 36 per cent 5 (very much). (2) "I increased my concern for community projects related to the course." On a scale from

1 to 5, 20.9 per cent marked 1 (no increase); 14.3 per cent 2; 36.8 per cent 3; 19.8 per cent 4; and 8.2 per cent 5 (great increase). (3) "I developed my ability to function creatively." On a scale from 1 to 5, 9.3 per cent indicated 1 (very much); 21.3 per cent 2; 45.6 per cent 3; 13 per cent 4; and 10.8 per cent 5 (very little).

Another response to instructional problems has been the creation of semi-autonomous instructional units—variously referred to as living-learning centers, inner colleges, satellite colleges, residential colleges, and subcolleges—on many large campuses during the past few years. Whatever the label, each one seems to have as its central purpose that of providing a liberal arts education. Gaff (1970) uses the term "cluster colleges" to refer to these units; he has examined many of them in depth and has sought to determine their similarities. Cluster colleges claim these advantages: Their size creates a close community in which personalized instruction is offered within the framework of warm student-faculty relations and facilitates experimentation with different approaches to learning which, in turn, increases the diversity of methods serving a diverse student body. Economies are attained because the small unit shares the facilities and services of the large campus. One of the most interesting and perhaps important features of the cluster college is its rejection of the assumptions that there is one liberal arts program and that all students must master the same body of knowledge and acquire the same intellectual methods to be liberally educated.

Summarizing the innovations of the cluster colleges, Gaff comments: "The dominant negative aspect of these changes is that they remove the arbitary barriers that have been erected between disciplines and departments, between students, faculty, and administrators, between the academic and social segments of students' lives, and between the campus and community. In a more positive vein, the changes are designed to foster an intellectual community that will help students to develop an integrated world view from the totality of their whole college experience" (pp. 61–62).

Research in several of the cluster colleges (Heist and Bilorusky, 1970) suggests that such schools appeal to students who differ in a number of ways from the masses. They tend to be nonauthoritarian in their thinking, open to new experiences and change, independent in judgment, and tolerant of ambiguous and frustrating experiences. Moreover, these students have "learned to learn" or at least seem ready to learn. Although most of these programs are so new and the research problems so formidable that their impact upon students is unknown, Gaff (1970) argues that "the cluster college concept emerges as a promising mechanism by which to place undergraduate liberal education once again at the center of the House of Intellect" (p. 238).

Two reports about two different types of cluster colleges also are available. The first one, a progress report from the Hutchins School of Liberal Studies of Sonoma State College (California), centers upon the first two years of operation and reflects some of the initially critical problems (Olson, 1971). The unit opened in the fall of 1969 with one hundred students; forty-five of these freshmen did not return as sophomores. Of the fifty-five who returned for their second year, thirty-five continued into the junior year. Of the sixty-seven freshmen entering in the fall of 1970, however, only 15 per cent did not return as sophomores.

While the faculty seemed to have little difficulty with freshmen in establishing mutual trust and understanding, such was not the case with sophomores (numerous anecdotal reports suggest that sophomores are almost universally a breed alone). Another problem arose in the seminars, the chief mode of instruction. Entirely too often to the liking of the faculty, students were ill-prepared, apathetic, and indifferent. This seminar problem should not be surprising to veteran faculty members, but it is surprising it finally has been admitted in print. The seminar has been lauded universally for so long that it has attained the status of a panacea for whatever ails the learning enterprise. But the praise for seminars and the usual few students in them may be much more the result of academic feather-bedding than of teaching-learning substance. The presumed effectiveness of the seminar is based upon at least one dubitable assumption, that the ability to lead a discussion directed toward learning is easy and any individual who is knowledgeable about a field of inquiry can do so without difficulty.

Indirect research evidence suggests that difficulties with seminars are widespread. One study (Pace, 1966) of some 100 institutions of higher learning in which students responded to the College and University Environment Scales (a questionnaire consisting of 150 items designed to determine student perceptions of many facets of their school) found that class discussions were rare in all institutions—not only public and private universities and state colleges but also both the prestigious liberal arts colleges and liberal arts colleges in general, in spite of the fact that the most prestigious ones often advertise their superiority along these lines.

The second report researches the changes in cluster college students over a four-year period (Shaw, 1970). During the academic year 1968–1969, 124 (92 per cent) of the graduating seniors from Justin Morrill College (a residential or living-learning center of Michigan State University) were interviewed in an effort to determine the degree to which both explicit and implicit goals of the center had been realized. Their responses were compared with those of twenty-four seniors graduating from the regular university programs. The two groups were matched on the basis of sex, academic major, and ability (as measured by a standarized test). The Justin Morrill College seniors, in contrast to the regular seniors:

97

(1) did not feel they had been restricted to utilizing only assigned class materials;

(2) needed and used resource and research materials;

(3) felt more comfortable and relaxed in their contacts with faculty members;

(4) believed that their education would be much more relevant to life following graduation;

(5) rated themselves significantly higher on listening skills;

(6) more often mentioned a faculty member as the person who had had a major influence upon their values; and

(7) were more concerned about social improvement activities.

There were several areas in which the groups responded comparably; there were no differeneces between the perceptions of the two in:

(1) concern and awareness for events of the world;

(2) feelings about their creativity and flexibility;

(3) alterations in their values from conservative toward liberal;

(4) participation in various activities of the university;

(5) admitting to having emotional or visceral reactions when encountering a person of a widely differing political or social persuasion; and

(6) trusting the words and actions of staff members of the university.

The most significant observation of the living-learning seniors was that to which they referred as a "lack of integration" of subject matter. They criticized lack of interrelatedness in the various academic disciplines. They charged that the traditional departmental boundaries had not been cut by the residential or cluster arrangement but had only been shifted, and for the benefit of the instructor, not the student.

Research reports about several of the cluster, or new, colleges—Johnston College, University of Redlands; Fairhaven College, Western Washington State College; The Residential College, University of Michigan; Justin Morrill College, Michigan State University; Callison College, University of Pacific; James Madison College, Michigan State University; and The University of California, Santa Cruz—contained in one monograph (edited by Dressel, 1971) are difficult to interpret because evaluation obviously means different things to different people. Nevertheless, two separate and global sorts of interpretations are offered in the volume. At one extreme, Dressel is bombastic in his criticisms. He argues in effect that many of the new programs are already in a state of decay as manifested by both loss of students and loss of faculty members. He praises the reports for their fullsome descriptiveness but condemns them because they offer little "evidence to justify a more extensive remodeling of undergraduate education." At the other extreme, Martin (1971b) concludes that noteworthy things are happening in many of the new colleges. He condemns the conventional research methodologies and the behavioral scientists who bring "shabby equipment" to the educative task.

The New College of the University of Alabama (1970), which opened in 1971, incorporates the features of many other cluster colleges and has added the contract. Rather than a single adviser, each student has a contract-advisery committee. The student is a voting member of the body which is composed of a faculty member and, at the student's option, a maximum of two other persons of his own choosing. These additional members may be members of the faculty, student body, or the off-campus community. The committee develops the program of education which constitutes the student's contract with New College.

Although research data are meager, at least two problems seem to be impeding the very laudatory efforts of cluster colleges to promote the integration of subject matter: narrowly trained disciplinary specialists who often have not integrated their own knowledge; and the assumption that a seminar composed of novices can be left to chance.

These problems can be attributed in part to the graduate schools, and it will be up to them to provide some salvation. The narrow discipline training of graduate students is well known; what is less well known is the cavalier fashion in which many of them are prepared for their teaching duties, either while in graduate school or as full-fledged faculty members. Dubin and Beisse (1967) state that there were 45,000 teaching assistants in 1963–1964, 31,000 serving in public universities. During 1965–1966, approximately 33 per cent of all undergraduate credit hours in the College of Literature, Science, and Arts at the University of Michigan, for example, were earned in classes taught by TA's; at the freshman and sophomore levels it was 45 per cent (Ericksen, 1965).

Interviews and questionnaires given to approximately 300 TA's from a total of 3,000 graduate students at the University of Rochester (Nowlis, Clark, and Rock, 1968) indicated their concerns: their departments were not sufficiently concerned with assisting them in the execution of their teaching duties; there were recurring conflicting interests among their instructional duties, their duties as students, and their duties as professional apprentices; they were either uncertain about their status within the university or certain that their status was ambiguous; they suffered a lack of self-confidence when facing undergraduates. Although statistical data are not included in the report, many undergraduates at the University of Rochester, while remarkably tolerant of TA's, expressed strong resentment of any conspicuous and persistent poor performance by them.

The most current and comprehensive data about TA's are furnished by Koen and Ericksen (1967). Questionnaires were sent to 193 departmental and administrative officers in the forty-four universities which supply about 90 per cent of the Ph.D. degrees. During visits to twenty of the schools structured interviews were conducted with 105 department chairmen, TA supervisors, and other faculty members. (Many of the departments are among the most highly rated in the nation.) Results of the study are based upon both the questionnaire and interview data from forty-two institutions. Seventy-one humanities, fourteen social science, and fifty-one natural science departments, plus ten professional schools and twenty-six administrative officers are represented.

TA's begin their instructional duties during their first graduate year in two-thirds of the departments. They are selected almost solely on the basis of their academic records and there is little concern with their competence in or potential for teaching. Although most departments claim that training is provided for this neophyte group, accredited faculty time for supervision and guidance is provided by less than one-third. Training varies from informal sessions to highly structured and rigorous endeavors—the latter are rare. There have been no changes during a ten-year period in about half of the training programs although undergraduate enrollments have doubled in this time. The most frequently utilized training procedure consists of perfunctory meetings of all new TA's followed throughout the term by "individual supervision." It appears, though, that "individual supervision" is more by chance than design; there are very few regularly scheduled meetings in most of the departments. "In most departments, teaching assistant-

101

ships are seen primarily as a means of providing undergraduate instruction and financial support for graduate students, rather than the explicit training of prospective college teachers. Most departments seem not to see the latter task as a major responsibility" (p. 50).

On our own campus, in March, 1969, questionnaire data were received from ninety-three teaching assistants, all of whom indicated they had primary responsibility for teaching a section or sections of a course. Eighty per cent stated they were provided orientation or guidance about the purposes of their course, what students were supposed to learn, and related matters; in the great majority of instances, however, only one or two hours were devoted to such issues. As for instruction about "how to lead class discussions" and "preparing and delivering lectures," 32 per cent and 17 per cent, respectively, answered in the affirmative. Again, in both instances, such instruction comprised a total of only one or two hours for most of the TA's.

The survey also revealed that 84 per cent of these teaching assistants prepared examination questions, scored test papers, and assigned final grades. Forty-three per cent indicated they received no guidance about testing and grading, while 24 per cent stated they had had one hour of instruction.

Williams and Richman (1971) provide some highly instructive information about what *consumers* want in the way of new Ph.D. faculty, thereby indicating alterations which are necessary in graduate programs (it seems likely that similar results would obtain in many other disciplines). Questionnaires were mailed to a randomly selected sample of 150 psychology department chairmen in colleges which did not offer the Ph.D. degree and to all the department chairmen in fifty "most selective" and "highly selective" colleges. Sixty-six per cent of the questionnaires were returned. The desires of the two groups of chairmen were remarkably similar. Approximately three-fourths either "disagreed" or "strongly disagreed" with this statement: "The typical graduate of a conventional Ph.D. program is well prepared to assume his teaching responsibilities." Approximately the same number either "agreed" or "strongly agreed" with each of these statements: "the ability to supervise and instruct undergraduates in their own research efforts is not emphasized enough in most graduate programs"; "an effective graduate program for college professors-to-be should orient the students as to their future responsibilities as general faculty members"; "there is a clear need for the development of Ph.D. programs aimed at the preparation of psychology professors for the four-year college" (p. 1,000ff).

Far be it from me to prescribe specific programs for graduate student training in teaching methods because it should be clear by now that my views are jaundiced (properly, of course). At the minimum, however, it seems mandatory that teaching assistants be provided some acquaintance with the "big issues" in higher education and training in some of the skills—how to lead a discussion and how to measure. There is a real danger that such efforts would become institutionalized and then we would have required methods courses. These would proliferate into methods for television and for lecturing and for small groups and for large groups and so on. Let me be perfectly clear, I am not proposing any of that.

We have made modest efforts at the University of Tennessee, Knoxville, in the direction of preparing graduate students for their instructional tasks. In the psychology department, a one-quarter three-hour seminar is required of all Ph.D. candidates. The issues discussed in this book as well as others—for example, academic governance—are pursued. A similar seminar is required of all candidates for the Master of Arts in College Teaching degree. This seminar reaches students in many fields—history, zoology, business, political science, and home economics, for example, and since the program is funded with foundation money, we have been able to bring leading authorities to the campus.

The English department has pioneered in assisting teaching assistants and young instructors in learning how to judge and mark themes. The most gratifying responses I have had (because they indicate the impact of these programs) have been long distance telephone calls or letters from graduates seeking literature references to particular instructional problems with which they are being confronted or which are being debated on their campus.

Perhaps the most ambitious program for teaching assistants has been developed at the University of Michigan (Koen, 1969); it is mentioned here because several departments participate—botany, history, philosophy, physics, and psychology. The program began in September, 1967, with three objectives: to develop a coordinated multidepartmental plan which would meet such criteria as efficiency, effectiveness, flexibility, and evolution; to raise the status and image of the graduate student teaching fellow; and to develop reliable instruments and procedures for assessing both teaching activities and the program. All departments maintain three levels of teaching assistants: third-year assistants are Instructors who assist second-year assistants, Teaching Fellows, who assist the first-year Trainees.

A seminar in the broad issues of higher education has been offered to graduate students at the University of Virginia for more than twenty years (Finger, 1969). Such topics as governance, academic freedom, types of institutions, and techniques of instruction are reviewed. The rationale for this program is summarized as follows: "Under attack as never before, the university cannot survive unaltered. It should be no surprise to today's professor if his influence is minimal, for his training has made him a subject-matter specialist, in no real sense a professional in higher education . . . perhaps our brightest hope is to provide a more balanced background for the professor of tomorrow" (p. 1048).

Korn (1972), in discussing instruction for the future, argues for a reversal in emphasis—from that of performing to that of planning. He maintains that planning has been neglected as a component of instruction even though planning is more important than execution or performance in the classroom. Quite consistent with my own thinking is his reasoning that designing a learning experience requires knowledge of the determinants of learning. Korn also sees this planning emphasis resulting in a better way to evaluate the effectiveness of instruction than do the popular methods based on performance, or what the professor does in the classroom (Miller, 1972).

At present, the movement from disciplinary instruction toward interdisciplinary integration is a feeble one. Very, very few students of the current eight million are profiting, especially those within the bulwark institutions, the large regional and state universities.

6

※※※※※※※※※※※※※※※※※※※※※※※※

What Do I
Have to Lose?

※※※※※※※※※※※※※※※※※※※※※※※※

The primary change I have advocated is abandonment of the faculty's surveillance role. As a corollary to that, I propose educational policy decisions must be based on research evidence, not tradition, hunch, or dogma. This aspect of the proposed shift is nothing more than an extension of a value system already deeply ingrained in faculty members—a value system which demands firm evidence for assertions about the

106

content of their own disciplines. In whatever ways the faculty role is eventually conceptualized, faculties must continue to make decisions about the "what" and the "how" of the curriculum—it is the latter to which this book has been addressed.

Many readers will carp about what they consider a lack of positive learning criteria to support many of my contentions. Such carping is to be hoped for and encouraged because it is most proper and because further searching should ensue during the process. The limited learning criteria in higher education constitute a fundamental part of the problem. As I plead for a research spirit, I mean a spirit that insists on more exalted criteria than grades and grade point averages—those fallible, unidimensional, and obfuscating creations designed to communicate about multidimensional, highly diversified, conglomerate phenomena.

An encouraging beginning toward the development of such measures has been made by the Center for the Study of Evaluation at the University of California, Los Angeles. Questionnaires have already been developed for students and alumni which explore a broad range of educational consequences including involvement in contemporary society and culture and awareness of some major changes taking place in American society. During 1969, a sample of alumni from the class of 1950 completed the scales (Pace and Milne, 1971) as did samples of freshmen and seniors from close to one hundred colleges and universities. Student data are now being analyzed, and, in the meantime, a kit (Pace, 1971) has been prepared which will facilitate on-going studies.

In my view, there are at least two paramount reasons for change in the direction of decisions being based on sound evidence. First, there is a need for consistency between what we believe and what we say; such concinnity would be a better model for students to imitate in their own pursuit of learning than the present somewhat disparate model. The new professorial model might increase the chances that students will learn to apply, generalize, or transfer. Second, forces afoot in the nation might result in very unpalatable alterations in the higher education system unless faculties take the initiative and do so with calculated rapidity. In this connection, the current cries about accountability are especially applicable. One of the taxpayer's chief sources of discontent with higher education stems from the conviction that his tax dollar is being misspent, that higher education consumes large amounts of public money but produces few measurable achievements (Smith, 1971). A study by the Brookings Institution (O'Neill, 1971), for example, demonstrated that between the mid-fifties and late sixties, there was virtually no change in costs per student credit hour in constant dollars. While most faculty members recoil from considering such mundane and shackling measures, we might ask ourselves: What measures can be substituted as contrary evidence, especially measures which might reveal cause-effect relationships?

As indicated in Chapter One, some legislatures already have reacted with strictures which may be damaging to the cause of learning. The faculty plight is exacerbated and made more difficult even for the educated lay person to understand by the fact that "less than 10 per cent of American faculties participate in professional research and publication, while even fewer engage in more routine community services" (Martin, 1971a, p. 4). Presumably, then, 90 per cent of us are engaged primarily in traditional teaching. I have not intended to suggest, in any degree, that students do not learn in colleges and universities—individual and group evidence of the fact of learning abounds for even the casual observer. Rather, I have intended to direct our attention toward fathoming the myriad of the "whys" of its occurrence and to at least some of the neglected aspects of it.

Although there is no need for further illustrations of

institutional resistance to change, if change is to occur, the process needs to be better understood by members of academe than it now seems to be. The Institute of Higher Education (Hefferlin, 1969) sought to determine some of the perceptions held by college and university staff members about forces for change within their own institutions. Long distance telephone interviews were conducted with 234 men and women—administrators, department chairmen, and professors (usually one from each group on each campus)—in one hundred colleges and universities. In effect, members of all groups perceived their group as the primary initiator of change. Neither faculty nor administrators felt they were impediments to change. These attitudes were conceptualized as "polarized provincialism" and provoked this conclusion: "But most important of all from our point of view, the fact of provinciality tends to cast doubt on the conviction of some faculty members and some administrators that the only answer to academic change lies on the one hand in greater faculty control or on the other in greater administrative initiative" (p. 104). Interestingly enough, 100 per cent of both administrators and department chairmen perceived students as trenchant forces for change, while none of the faculty saw the students in that capacity.

Hefferlin (1969) has extracted from the voluminous literature on organizational change several major conclusions which may be reviewed as a provocative base for further thought:

(1) "Organizations are inherently passive" (p. 10) in that they tend to be efficient arrangements for the continual providing of a service. Furthermore, they are hierarchically structured in that some members have more power and authority than others, and those with power can remain unresponsive to many pleas over long periods of time.

(2) "Organizations tend toward institutionalization and ritualism" or means to ends become ends in themselves.

109

Over a period of time, procedures "assume a sacred quality [and] the methods for achieving a goal slowly come to be considered the goal itself" and appear irrevocable. Grades and grade point averages are an especially good example of the "goal itself" (p. 11).

(3) "Organizations that are livelihoods for people tend to come to exist only as livelihoods for these people" (p. 12). Here is the issue of vested interests; resistance is highest whenever one's own livelihood is threatened (and understandably so). Surrendering the surveillance role should in no way threaten vested faculty interests, however. Instead, it should enliven those interests.

(4) "The maintenance of institutional effectiveness or achievement (such as student's learning) is only one problem that organizations face in order to survive" (p. 12). Whenever large numbers of people work together, numerous problems arise, especially those of an interpersonal nature. Since these must be attended to, time and attention are diverted from the central task. The budget and attendant financial matters are perennially time-comsuming, and women's rights, students' rights, and the rights of nonacademic personnel have been frequent distractions.

While the previous statements apply to organizations in general, academic institutions have unique characteristics which additionally retard change.

(5) "Their purposes and support are basically conservative" (p. 13). Given an institution whose primary purpose is transmission of the cultural heritage, whose governing bodies are frequently an elite group, and whose academic disciplines were founded in the past, one should not be surprised that the institution is wary of change.

(6) "The educational system is vertically fragmented" (p. 13). Many academic practices are dominated by the graduate schools. For example, graduate faculties and deans have

opposed pass-fail grading for undergraduates on the grounds that such grading would interfere with sound selection procedures. This domination has existed for many years in spite of the fact that a very small proportion of undergraduates have been destined for graduate school.

(7) "Faculty members have observed their vocation for years as students before joining it" (p. 14). When someone observes the teacher's role for twenty years before assuming the role himself, he already knows what his role is.

(8) "The ideology of the academic profession treats professors as independent professionals" (p. 15). This ideology is deeply entrenched and is protected with more or less constant vigilance. Research is an anomaly, in that cooperation and criticism are expected and sought; instruction, however, is isolated from even constructive criticism.

(9) "Academics are skeptical about the idea of efficiency in academic life" (p. 15). The myth that the teaching-learning endeavor is a mysterious process encourages the attitude that the results defy measurement. Since the end product is so unquestionably "good," cost need be of little consequence.

(10) "Academic institutions are deliberately structured to resist precipitant change" (p. 16). There is a diffusion of power and authority, and major educational policy decisions must work upward through a maze, commonly known as buck-passing. The possibilities for modifying and even blocking alterations exist at every level of the maze.

According to Hefferlin (1969), there is general agreement that there are at least three dominant and interwoven sources for academic change. The first is financial support. Many new programs cost money and are resisted vigorously if the money must be taken from existing programs. This financial fact helps to explain why academic changes most often originate outside the educational system itself; the money comes from external sources. A case in point on our own campus is the money provided by the Alumni Association for outstanding teaching awards. A faculty committee, in developing a very elaborate and comprehensive procedure for selecting three annual recipients, in turn helped to promote additional efforts (primarily at the instigation of the Student Senate) to evaluate teaching. A second source of change is people, either individually or collectively, who serve as persuaders and advocates. These, too, often come from the outside—new faculty members and students, for instance, who bring differing viewpoints to the campus. The third source is the receptivity of the particular institution—some of them seem to be ready for change while others are stagnant and resistant. The ingredients of institutional vitality are not at all clear and take different forms in different places.

Ladd (1970) attempts to ferret out a definitive understanding of the dynamics of change by examining eleven colleges and universities (Columbia; Swarthmore; Brown; Duke; Michigan State; Stanford; Wesleyan; University of California, Berkeley and Los Angeles; New Hampshire University; and Toronto University), all of which had conducted studies of their own problems and made proposals for educational policy reforms. Formal reports were examined, and at subsequent visits to the campuses, interviews were held with a variety of individuals who were involved with the events immediately related to the studies. At each school an attempt was made to determine: the origins of the study, the composition of the study group, the processes of the study, and recommendations and implementation. Several tentative conclusions were drawn from the resulting case histories:

(1) Except when faced with severe pressure or the threat of it, the ability of our institutions of higher education to respond to change is "frighteningly limited."

(2) The study-and-report technique, so common in colleges and universities, did not effectively promote the accep-

tance of a need for change or "enthusiasm in the development of new policies." At two of the schools, Duke University and Swarthmore College, most of the recommendations were adopted quickly but "there was relatively widespread acceptance of the idea that changes were needed before the studies began." Conversely, studies were begun at Columbia College, Michigan State University, and the University of New Hampshire because a senior administrator wanted to promote changes. "The extent of the changes made as a result of the studies was rather limited."

(3) Student pressure on the faculties at Brown University and the University of Toronto seemed to be the important impetus in implementing changes in educational policies. The students at Brown University had an extremely clever leader, and their pressure on the faculty was constant and unrelenting.

(4) Nearly all the committees on the separate campuses worked together effectively even though there was no consistent pattern in the composition of these committees. Neither the cooperativeness nor the composition seemed to have any relation to acceptance of the study.

(5) All the study committees made a great variety of efforts to promote involvement across their campuses, but participation "did not seem to expand greatly the likelihood of bringing about change." "After the Macpherson report at Toronto had been public for nearly a year, Dean Allen announced in a faculty meeting that a committee was to draw up and present to the faculty in two weeks' time legislation to implement certain of the Macpherson proposals. A number of faculty members took to the floor to complain of the short time allowed to consider 'such momentous changes'" (p. 203).

Such lack of commitment and of active involvement in academic governance has been examined carefully at one large midwestern university (Dykes, 1968). Interviews were held with a 20 per cent randomly selected sample of faculty members (stratified by rank) of the College of Liberal Arts and Sciences. On the one hand, the respondents maintained that faculty members should have determining voices about educational functions, while, on the other, they placed participation in such decision-making at the bottom of their list of priorities even though they were persistently unwilling to delegate responsibility for decision-makng to others. A second finding was a serious misperception of reality. In effect, the interviewees did not know the processes by which academic decisions were made on their own campus; as a consequence, there was unnecessary suspicion and distrust. General reading and observation lead me to believe that these findings are not isolated ones. (In light of the apathy of the general citizenry toward participation in their own local governments, what do the great washed have over the great unwashed?)

(6) Strong leadership was essential. From whom it came did not seem to be of any great moment—it came from the president at Swarthmore College; from a dean at the University of Toronto; from a faculty member at the University of California, Berkeley; and from a student at Brown University. The most sweeping reforms were at the first and last mentioned schools.

(7) There appeared to be a negative correlation between size and change—the larger the institution, the less the change: "It is quite obvious that we can have personnel policies and purchasing policies and library policies in any university, however large. All large bureaucracies have these. What is less obvious after examination of these studies is whether or not large institutions can have *educational* policies—whether the American tradition of giant institutions has not, in the case of higher education, reached the point of diminishing returns" (p. 209).

This distinction between housekeeping and educational

114

policies strikes me as being of profound significance for all of us who wish to promote learning. Time after time, when serving on a universitywide educational policy committee, I have witnessed the representatives from one college quash the proposals from another. And why not? Different colleges have different purposes.

Mooney (1963) offers some theories which help to account for the resistance to change in the large universities. He argues that leadership is no longer possible because of size and, more importantly, because of the impact of both federal and foundation research monies on the lines of authority. In some cases, the huge sums of money which are obtained by faculty members and which remain under their control have created, in effect, a group on the campus which is not subject to local administrative and faculty governance. As a result, serious schisms have developed so that faculties are more fractionated now than ever before along the lines of research and teaching.

The following conversation overheard at an informal gathering of dedicated faculty members is very pertinent to the subject of change because it emphasizes the fact that principles and procedures of change must vary: "A large university of 25,000 students is qualitatively different from a college of 500 students; one is a dinosaur and the other a shrew." First rejoinder: "And dinosaurs are extinct." Second rejoinder: "And shrews work in the dark."

In still another attempt to understand change, faculties were studied—first in considerable depth at Metro University (Evans, Smith, and Colville, 1962) and later, to lesser degrees, in nine others. Conducted in the early 1960s, the studies utilized the possible adoption of instructional television (ITV) as the issue for consideration by faculties and found a relatively low opinion of the medium throughout the faculty as a whole. Then, fifty-five faculty members who were favorably disposed

115

toward it were identified, and sixty-five were selected who were hostile to it. All members of these two groups were studied via several attitude questionnaires and by personal interviews. The pro-ITV professors came most frequently from engineering-technology, communication arts, and business. The anti-ITV professors came most frequently from the social sciences, physical-biological sciences, humanities, and education. The pro-ITV professors tended to be more tolerant people, to possess a greater tolerance for change, and to be more willing to use a greater variety of techniques and procedures in both instruction and evaluation. Members of this group tended to be isolated in their departments for their views about ITV; but they seemed to be able to maintain the strength of their convictions. In a sense, they were less academically oriented than the anti-ITV professors in that they were also concerned about the social aspects of the university. The anti-ITV professors expressed fears about job loss and about the creation of a "star" system and anxiety about the possibility of their exposure through television to the criticism of their colleagues. These individuals knew where they fitted into an "academically ordered world" and rejected anything which threatened to dilute the traditional university and their roles in it. The anti-ITVers tended to be members of departments in which their views were shared by their colleagues.

Further data were gathered from nine additional schools (Evans, 1968)—Hofstra, Michigan State, Southern Methodist, Texas Christian, Trinity, Washington University, San Francisco State, State University of New York at Buffalo, and the University of Pittsburgh. Interviews were held, sometimes in private and sometimes in groups with both faculty members and administrators; provocative questions were asked. In general, the findings about attitudes toward instructional television confirmed those already obtained at Metro University; the predominant attitude was one of hostility.

Attitudes toward the medium seemed to be uncorrelated with the structure of the institution or other characteristics of it— size, urban or rural, sponsorship, and experience or inexperience with ITV.

There was marked similarity among the reasons for opposition across the ten schools. Some of the reasons advanced were rational and objective, but most of them were irrational and emotional. The tortured reasoning often employed was illustrated by the remarks of a very productive biological scientist who was truly innovative in his discipline. While discussing the point that essentially the same pattern of instruction has been maintained in universities since their inception, he reasoned that "the persistence of traditional methods actually indicates their superiority."

It will be recalled that in the studies of acceptance or nonacceptance of advanced placement, many faculty members insisted that it was fine in other courses but not in theirs (see Chapter Two). A similar resistance was manifested toward ITV; for example, a math professor and a music professor each argued that although the other could profitably use the medium, he could not because of the importance of providing feedback to the student. The similar ring of the resistance to both advanced placement and instructional television suggests a generic view of the teaching role, a view which is based upon many years of unquestioned tradition. Once again, we see manifestations of the pervasiveness of the emotional aura which surrounds instruction. The aura seems to be more deeply impregnated in the area of instruction than in any other human activity. Even the Freudian mechanisms of defense seem unconvincing as explanations, except in isolated cases.

The latest investigation (Fashing and Deutsch, 1971) about changes on particular campuses was conducted between 1968 and 1971. The universities of California at Berkeley and Los Angeles, the University of Oregon, San Francisco State and

Alternatives to the Traditional

Western Washington State colleges, and Stanford University were visited on several occasions and for varying periods of time. Lengthy interviews were held with representative individuals—faculty, administrators, and students—and numerous reports and documents were consulted. Seeking information about the sources of and support for change, the investigation revealed that students played significant roles in the changes which occurred on those campuses, and the faculty was a neutral force, at best, and more often the center of resistance to change.

Following careful analysis of the resistance of United States Navy officialdom to the introduction of continuous-aim firing devices on battleships around 1900, devices which had been demonstrated to increase gunnery accuracy by 3000 per cent, Morison (1961) offers penetrating explanations for the universality of resistance to change and cogent suggestions for overcoming it. His findings can be generalized to the academic scene. Morison proposes that conflicts arose over innovation because of the different identifications held by men in varying positions and with varying responsibilities. Thus some men identified themselves with their creations and obtained satisfaction from the thing itself. Such satisfaction prevented them from thinking about the ultimate use or defects of the object. Other men identified with a way of life they found comfortable and satisfying. Still other individuals identified themselves as "rebellious" and gained satisfacton from challenging the status quo. In general, most individuals were victims of limiting identifications, which prevented them from seeing the forest for the trees.

Morison suggests that any group should define for itself a "grand object" and "see to it that that grand object is communicated to every member of the group" (p. 604). He reasons that acceptance of the grand object would serve to unite members of the group and increase the acceptability of

118

any change that might promote it. (Perhaps the grand object in higher education has been research, especially during the past twenty years; the grand object now might become the promotion of learning.)

Several strategies for fostering change are advanced by Maguire (1971): the new proposal should not be a radical departure but a modification of existing practices; push for change should be gradual; the group seeking change should exercise self-discipline and agree among themselves about priorities; the support of marginal members of the institution— for example, alumni—should be enlisted; and a unit should be established (and adequately financed) to handle research and development.

In this last regard, several large institutions have created units which have as their primary concern the improvement of teaching-learning (these are listed in the Appendix). These offices vary in size, funding, and scope of their activities and pursue their charge in various ways. The example with which I am most familiar, the Learning Research Center of The University of Tennessee, Knoxville, was created in September, 1965, largely as a result of recommendations from the 1961 accreditation self-study. The Center operates under the auspices of the vice-chancellor for academic affairs; its primary mission is encouraging faculty debate and exploration of substantive learning issues. Information is systematically and regularly supplied to the entire staff, and funds are supplied to individual faculty members for the examination of instructional ideas. The guiding philosophy of the Center is respect for faculty ethos, especially that which holds that faculty members are independent professionals. Persuasion is the only tactic employed, and it is applied within the framework of faculty values. I, myself, hold certain truths to be self-evident. The Center is assisted in its work by an Advisory Committee consisting of faculty members from all the colleges and one or two adminis-

119

trative officials. This body carries more weight with the faculty than one individual could; it assists in the implementation of ideas of the director, and, in turn, the staff of the Center assists subcommittees of that group in executing their tasks.

Information is supplied in several ways, and I am convinced that a variety of information is essential. Faculty members on a large campus are a heterogeneous and busy lot; no topic has universal appeal. Moreover, one must be careful not to supply too much reading material; if the selection seems overwhelmingly large or the length of a given article is too long, the material ends in the wastebasket.

Funds for undergraduate instructional research are supplied to the faculty through what have been dubbed mini-mini grants (generally around two hundred dollars, although we have found that considerable mileage is possible from even smaller amounts than that). Red tape is kept to a bare minimum; proposals are no more than one page in length and are usually acted upon within a few hours of receipt. All grants require measurement of the effect of the idea upon instruction. This effect must be objectively judged; the opinion of the one faculty member is unacceptable evidence. And now I must mince my words delicately, measurement of instructional results is a foreign concept to many faculty applicants, even a few in the hard sciences. In the main, these small sums of money help the instructor in the execution of his tasks. Many faculty members who are suspicious of higher education research specialists find their own research results convincing, and the results of a study are likely to spread within the department in which it was conducted. A few examples of mini-mini grant projects follow.

Agricultural Biology. Color slides depicting the step-by-step performance necessary during laboratory exercises were produced. Slides of diseased specimens and photomicrographs

120

of diseased tissue and pathogenic organisms were prepared. All these were available for students to use prior to their laboratory work. It was found that structures to be studied in fresh tissues were more easily recognized after viewing the color slides and less time was spent by instructors in aiding students in routine searches for objectives. Better students (A's and B's) devoted between twenty-five and thirty minutes to studying the color slides, while the other students utilized them less than twenty minutes; cause-effect is not implied.

Architecture, Introductory Design. Twenty-one students participated in a special design course set up to determine the effect on students of the complete conception, execution, and construction of a project. Initially each student was requested to isolate a design problem which met the following requirements: it involved a "structure" for human use; it conformed to all applicable health and safety regulations; it possessed some degree of civic worth; it could be constructed by members of the class; and it could not cost more than two hundred dollars (the amount of the mini-mini grant). Each student submitted a complete solution to his problem and included graphic presentations, costs, and so on. After a jury had selected five projects for further development, four-man student teams refined each solution. Reviews of all solutions by faculty members led to selection of a piece of therapeutic equipment as the class project. The final product was donated to a children's orthopedic hospital.

During subsequent quarters, these twenty-one students were dispersed in a number of other architecture courses. Faculty members made these judgments about them: (1) In a section of thirty-seven students in traditional design courses, seven out of ten of the experimental ones ranked above the class average; four excelled. (2) In a section of thirty-two students developing graphic solutions to technical problems, both the experimental ones excelled. (3) In a section of thirty-five students individually designing and constructing furniture, six of eight experimental students ranked above average. (4) In a section of twenty-six students engaged in designing medical facilities, eight of nine experimental students ranked above average and four excelled. (5) In a section of twenty students designing a solution to an abstract problem with complex requirements, two of six experimental students ranked only average; the other four either failed or did not complete their work. The evaluations revealed that the experimental students transferred their learning to similar problems better than did traditional ones. Their failure with a dissimilar problem, an abstract one, leaves many unanswered questions about instruction.

Education, History, and Philosophy. An attitude scale covering racial prejudice, jingoism, money-orientedness, dishonesty, conformity, religious dogmatism, antiliberalism, and authoritarianism was administered (on a pre- and posttest basis) to nine sections of students taught by seven different professors. The statistical design was analysis of covariance. Two of the sections, which emphasized humanistic reading materials, multimedia dynamics, active student participation, individualized assignments, sensitivity experience, and existential commitment to values, showed significant changes in values. Three of the nonexperimental sections showed changes in one or two categories of values, while the remaining four nonexperimental sections showed no changes in any of the categories.

Family Living Management. One section of students played a life career simulation game as part of their course work; a second section did not use the game. A pre- and posttest design was utilized for three tests—comprehension, application, and knowledge. There were only slightly higher gains by the game group than by the nongame one in all three areas. It was concluded that the game did not affect the cognitive elements of the course. Students who felt the game should be incorporated into the course outnumbered those who felt it was not worth the time by five to one.

Journalism. Two sections were given special writing assignments in addition to their regular class work. One group (A) was informed that its work would form a special publication devoted to the future of the University. The other group (B) was informed that its special assignment was a term paper. Students in Group A spent twice as much time on their writing as did those in Group B. With one exception, the papers in Group A needed little or no rewriting; moreover, all deadlines were met. Students in Group B were casual about their work, and only two of them met deadlines. One student, when questioned about a missed deadline and the poor quality of work, replied: "Well, you'd just put it away somewhere, so why should I put myself out?" Another student explained: "It's only a one-hour course." Three practicing newsmen, without knowing the nature of the assignments, were asked to judge the work of both groups. The judges agreed that papers from Group A (with one exception) were near professional standards. They agreed that all papers in Group B (except two) were of poor quality and needed rewriting. (The papers from Group A were published.) The results of this study may help to explain the results of the English composition study cited in Chapter One. The students in Group A apparently felt their work had an important purpose. Those in Group B and the composition study may not have felt the same.

Mathematics, Calculus. This study was reported in Chapter One and is mentioned again because it generated an unanticipated result—an enormous amount of conversation in the Mathematics Department about teaching and learning. Discussions of teaching methods, grading practices, and so on, became the order of the day among both graduate students and faculty members; previously such discussions had been almost nonexistent. (The mini-mini grant was for only twenty-five dollars; the money was spent for duplicating materials and postage.)

Mathematics, General. In isolation, brief counseling, weekly positive reenforcement by a counselor (an advanced graduate student), and peer tutoring (by high-ability mathematics undergraduates) did not increase the performance of risk students (those with high school math averages below C and scoring below 20 on the mathematics section of the ACT). A combination of brief individual counseling and peer tutoring, however, produced significant increases in performance on math tests.

Physics, Introductory. Several internal reorganizations were made in two large sections each quarter in an effort to increase teaching-learning effectiveness. In essence, each section contained three experimental groups: Approximately thirty students sat at the front of the center section of the lecture room and interacted with the instructor; for another group, largely upperclassmen, class attendance was entirely optional; the remainder of the class was required to attend on a regular basis—they listened to and observed the recitation group but could not interrupt the instructor. According to postcourse questionnaires, students preferred the groups into which they had been placed or which they had chosen. Members of the "regular" group seemed content with their passive role and stated their preference for observing a live recitation rather than a television lecture. The recitation group wanted to continue the arrangement in successive quarters, and the option students felt that even more students should be included in that group (approximately two-thirds of them seldom or never attended class). The recitation students, as a whole, scored higher on examinations than did students in the other two groups; such data as ACT scores indicated that better students

124

tended to select this approach. There was a higher concentration of Cs in the option than in the regular group.

Psychology. Funds were used to develop an association test intended to measure the learning of content. Several studies, including one dissertation (Jennings, 1968), revealed that groups of students pursuing the same subject matter but working under different instructors produced quite different associations to basic concepts. The association test shows promise of becoming a very sensitive classroom measuring device.

A procedure was developed to facilitate direct study of student attention in the classroom. Each of three graduate student observers monitored twenty students in a televised introductory course. The checklist consisted of four categories of student attending and nonattending behaviors. A fourth observer divided his time among the three groups to obtain reliabilities; rate of agreement between observations ranged from 75 to 100 per cent. Marked differences were observed in attending and nonattending frequencies for various course topics. For example, films were associated with high frequencies of attending behavior, and lectures on learning and conditioning were associated with high frequencies of nonattending behavior.

Zoology. The department considered whether student enthusiasm and learning would be increased by having live specimens for study in invertebrate zoology. Accordingly, live animals were purchased from various biological supply companies. Questionnaires administered at the end of the quarter revealed greater interest on the part of the group studying live animals as contrasted with those studying animals in a preserved state; however, a specially constructed final examination did not reveal any increase in learning.

These small sums of money have helped demonstrate to the faculty that the administration means what it says about

125

improving instruction. The money also has helped reduce the tedium that is so often involved in making any change. One of the realities that emerged from these small-scale studies is the necessity for multiple assessment criteria. And, while many of the mini-mini grant investigations revealed no differences in learning (as measured by conventional tests), others reported differences in interest aroused, time saved by the instructor, limitations of a particular approach, and so on.

Still other activities of the Center include informing faculty members about regional or national meetings they may wish to attend and in some cases providing the necessary financial support. For example, in September 1971, five faculty members attended the conference "Justice for Freshmen," which was held in Cleveland; and in October 1971 two attended the "Conference on the Keller Plan," held at the Massachusetts Institute of Technology. Such activities seem to be far more effective than when I, alone, attend and render a report upon return.

Determining the effects of the Learning Research Center on the campus is difficult, and I must guard against seeing what I want to see. Changes which have occurred over a span of seven years cannot be determined easily, and many of our faculty members are alert and progressive and do not need any assistance. As part of the accreditation self-study of 1971, however, faculty members were asked whether they agreed that "the activities of the Learning Research Center have helped improve the teaching-learning process." Seven hundred twenty-one responded as follows: 46 per cent agreed, 45 per cent were undecided, and 9 per cent disagreed.

Without meaning to be presumptuous, let me offer a few guiding principles for those institutions which contemplate the creation of an instructional research center. The academic discipline of the leader or director is unimportant—his or her interest in fundamental educational issues should be the chief determinant in selection. The person chosen for such a position should have the respect of the faculty and possess all the academic credentials. The position need not be full time, especially on a small campus, but it should be funded adequately; the director should not have to beg funds each time an idea strikes him. Finally, if small sums of money are to be awarded to the faculty for research in their teaching, decisions about each application should be made by a faculty committee, not by an individual.

The dynamics of institutional change are exceptionally complex. Limited and provincial views are impediments to change, and the one vaunted technique for bringing about change—study and report—has been demonstrated to be ineffective. Most local units created especially for promoting change have been in existence such a short time that their long-range effectiveness is unclear. It does seem reasonable, though, that funded and systematic efforts are more likely to succeed than is traditional trial and error.

7

❈❈❈❈❈❈❈❈❈❈❈❈❈❈❈❈❈❈

Epilogue

❈❈❈❈❈❈❈❈❈❈❈❈❈❈❈❈❈❈

The traditional conditions for promoting learning, so long cherished by so many—small classes, discussions, frequent class meetings—have been found wanting; each one is related only peripherally to learning, and collectively their endearment has aided in obscuring the central learning issues. There are many explanations for the fact that traditional conditions are losing their attraction but perhaps the simplest is that they have become ends in themselves, little more than perfunctory rituals for both faculty and students, but especially the latter. There is a vacuous quality to the efforts of many college "learners," and their mechanical parroting and puppeting as they continue in the accustomed routines do not fix learning more or less permanently. To learn, in any important sense, requires an inordinate investment of one's self and one's energy.

At first glance, a few studies have raised disturbing doubts about what many of us have believed are fundamental principles of learning—feedback and practice. The evidence is sketchy and caution in its use is in order, but at least three explanations for such findings appeal to me. First, the research results apply to groups of students rather than to individuals; much of significance may be submerged in the statistics. The next national research emphasis should be examination of the learning styles of individual students. Second, feedback is a nebulous notion (one among many) and apparently is not too well understood. If feedback is to promote learning, it must be definitive. If all a student is interested in knowing is whether he passed a course, a letter grade is sufficient. The type necessary may be related to the student's level of mastery; perhaps advanced students supply their own feedback. Finally, how feedback is delivered may vary from field to field. For example, one study (Hodgkinson, Walter, and Coover, 1968) in the teaching of English composition suggests that the ability to accept errors is much better with the ear than with the eye in that subject. A third explanation for the results about feedback and practice is that motivation is a powerful force in higher-order learning; if students do not wish to learn what we offer, then, no matter what principles are applied, learning will not occur.

Observations on my own campus and conversations with my colleagues across the nation lead me to believe that between one-third and one-half the student population is enrolled in college because society has demanded it of them or because society provides few other systems within which they may mature. The platitude that "faculties should motivate students" is shallow and misleading. Superficial motivation is relatively easy; sustained motivation is all but impossible. Alan Pifer, president of the Carnegie Corporation, has declared that the custody of reluctant students is an improper role for institutions of higher learning (1972). This is a belated but beknighted declaration; let us hope that allowance is made for the custodial function in any demands from the public for accountability.

Inextricably bound to all higher education rituals is the symbol scramble. Many of society's most influential private and public employers see higher education as a personnel selection device in which the "good" are separated from the "undesirable." Such public pressure helps explain many idiosyncracies of higher education and especially the restricted and restricting procedures for testing and grading. The most sensible proposal I have encountered for halting the symbol scramble is contained in the *Newman Report* (Newman, 1971) which recommends the creation of regional examining universities. These would offer no courses but would administer equivalency examinations so that individuals could receive credit independent of how their knowledge and skills were acquired. Newman foresees that such an endeavor would destroy the credential monopoly now enjoyed by the institutions responsible for education.

Faculties and students would be free to pursue learning on many levels; critical thinking and respect for differences of opinion should proliferate when neither student nor teacher is under the thumb of a grading system. Local evaluation would continue but in a more flexible form and serving its true purpose of improving student performance.

In my own classroom experiences, students are of two types: the timid conformists who never disagree with or challenge my assessment of their answers to test questions and the aggressive activists who fight my every judgment, not for the purpose of learning but for the purpose of gaining points to-

130

ward *the* grade. I sympathize with both types and anguish about a system which forces students and faculty members to be adversaries rather than learning partners. Scholars, as I understand the term, are supposed to be critics; scholarly instructors in higher education should help students learn to be critics. The present pseudo-licensing function now all but prevents an instructor from fulfilling this role in that his answers are final and exact for some students and signals for a displaced battle for others.

While there is a sustaining emotional aura within academe about instructional procedures and arrangements, there is a welling emotional confusion without; the emotional reactions of the public toward higher education are interpreted by Martin (1971c), however, as an expression of uncertainty about society's values, not as a plea for a return to traditional instructional conservatism. The challenge from the public, then, is that higher education exercise leadership in preparing society for the future. Current steps toward the creation of flexible routes to learning are one manifestation of leadership, as are beginning efforts to relate disciplines. The most important guiding principle is that what a student knows is more important than how he learned it. Finally, the heretofore exclusive domains are being opened to all who can benefit from the wares therein. Youth will benefit from exposure to and interaction with their elders, and faculties will benefit because helping people who *want* to learn is fulfilling and rewarding.

How can institutions be reorganized to allow educational issues to become paramount and theories about undergraduate learning a reality?

The fact that a campus ombudsman reports (Rust, 1969) that slightly over half his work involves disputes between faculty members and students about academic matters should tell us that conditions for learning need a thorough reexamination.

Alternatives to the Traditional

How can undergraduate faculty members be helped to oppose graduate school domination of curricular affairs?

Many undergraduate courses are based on the proposition that most students will either major in the field or attend graduate school. Statistics reveal that a majority of students do not attend graduate school.

How do we introduce and encourage the weaning process so that responsibility for learning is assumed by the student?

Now that eighteen is the age of majority, it may not be long until students turn their attention to academic rights as they have already to housing rights. It is my impression, though, that many of them are unready to assume responsibility for their own learning. Furthermore, I am afraid our efforts in aiding their independence will be hampered by current public demands for accountability; but I repeat: efficient teaching by the faculty does not necessarily promote sufficient learning by the students.

Appendix: Instructional Research and Development Units

UNIVERSITY OF CINCINNATI
Institute for Research and
Training in Higher
Education
Hanna Hall, Room 372
Cincinnati, Ohio 45221
COLORADO STATE UNIVERSITY

Administration Building
Room 110
Fort Collins, Colorado 80521
UNIVERSITY OF DELAWARE
Academic Planning and
Evaluation
Newark, Delaware 19711

Appendix

FLORIDA STATE UNIVERSITY
Research and Development
Center
Tallahassee, Florida 32306

UNIVERSITY OF GEORGIA
Instructional Research and
Development
Psychology Building
Athens, Georgia 30601

GEORGIA INSTITUTE OF
TECHNOLOGY
Office of Evaluation Studies
Atlanta, Georgia 30332

UNIVERSITY OF ILLINOIS
Office of Instructional
Resources
205 South Goodwin
Urbana, Illinois 61801

MASSACHUSETTS INSTITUTE OF
TECHNOLOGY
Educational Research Center
Cambridge, Massachusetts
02139

MCGILL UNIVERSITY
Centre for Learning and
Development
Montreal 110, Quebec

UNIVERSITY OF MICHIGAN
Center for Research on
Learning and Teaching
109 East Madison Street
Ann Arbor, Michigan 48104

MICHIGAN STATE UNIVERSITY
Instructional Development
Service
East Lansing, Michigan
48823

UNIVERSITY OF MINNESOTA
Center for Research in
Human Learning
Minneapolis, Minnesota
55455

STATE UNIVERSITY OF NEW
YORK
Planning Studies
Stony Brook, New York
11790

NORTHWESTERN UNIVERSITY
Center for the Teaching
Professions
Evanston, Illinois 60201

OHIO STATE UNIVERSITY
Office of Educational
Development
500 W. 12th Avenue
Columbus, Ohio 43210

UNIVERSITY OF PITTSBURGH
Division of Instructional
Experimentation
416 Cathedral of Learning
Pittsburgh, Pennsylvania
15213

UNIVERSITY OF TENNESSEE,
KNOXVILLE
Learning Research Center
Alumni Hall
Knoxville, Tennessee 37916

UNIVERSITY OF TOLEDO
Center for the Study of
Higher Education
Toledo, Ohio 43606

UNIVERSITY OF UTAH
Center to Improve Learning

and Instruction
308 W. Milton Bennion Hall
Salt Lake City, Utah 84111
UTAH STATE UNIVERSITY

Improvement of Instruction
Office
Merrill Library, Room 202
Logan, Utah 84321

Several medical schools have created these units; specific information can be obtained from:

ASSOCIATION OF AMERICAN
  MEDICAL COLLEGES
Division of Educational

Measurement and Research
2530 Ridge Avenue
Evanston, Illinois 60201

References

American College Testing Program. *College Student Profiles: Norms for the ACT Assessment.* Iowa City: American College Testing Program, 1966.

ANDERSON, J. J. *History of Western Civilization—Audio-Tutorial Style.* Rockville, Md.: Montgomery College, n.d.

ANDREWS, G. J. Assistant to the director, Southern Association of Colleges and Schools, Atlanta. Letter to author, December 15, 1971.

The Assembly on University Goals and Governance. *A First Report.* Cambridge, Mass.: American Academy of Arts and Sciences, 1971.

ASTIN, A. "Higher Education for the Future: Reform or More of the Same?" *Regional Action,* 1971, *22*(4), 2–3.

References

AULD, R. B. "The Cooperative Education Movement—Early Years." *Journal of Cooperative Education,* 1971, *7*(2), 7–9.

BAKER, W. H. "A Study of Selected Characteristics of Cooperative Engineering Students." *Journal of Cooperative Education,* 1969, *5*(2), 40–48.

BARRETT, J. S. President, Spartanburg Junior College. Letter to author, December 10, 1971.

BASKIN, S. *University Without Walls: A Proposal for an Experimental Degree Program in Undergraduate Education.* Yellow Springs, Ohio: Union for Experimenting Colleges and Universities, Antioch College, 1970.

BASKIN, S. *University Without Walls: A First Report.* Yellow Springs, Ohio: Union for Experimenting Colleges and Universities, Antioch College, 1972.

BERG, I. *Education and Jobs: The Great Training Robbery.* New York: Praeger, 1970.

BLACKWELL, T. E. *College Law: A Guide for Administrators.* Washington, D.C.: American Council on Education, 1961.

BORN, D. G. *Instructor Manual for Development of a Personalized Instruction Course.* Salt Lake City: Center to Improve Learning and Instruction, University of Utah, 1970.

BOWERS, W. J. *Student Dishonesty and its Control in College.* Cooperative Research Project 1672, USOE. New York: Bureau of Applied Social Research, Columbia University, 1964.

BRUNER, J. S. *The Process of Education.* Cambridge: Harvard University Press, 1960. By permission of the publisher.

CALIFANO, J. A., JR. *The Student Revolution: A Global Confrontation.* New York: Norton, 1969.

Carnegie Commission on Higher Education, *Less Time, More Options: Education Beyond the High School.* New York: McGraw-Hill, 1971.

Carnegie Corporation of New York. *Annual Report, 1971.* New York: Carnegie Corporation of New York, 1972.

CARPENTER, C. R. "What are the Most Effective Methods of Improved Instruction, With Special Reference to Individ-

References

ual Work Programs?" In G. K. Smith (Ed.), *Current Issues in Higher Education*. Washington: Association for Higher Education, 1959.

CASSERLY, P. L. *College Decisions on Advanced Placement*. Princeton: Educational Testing Service, Research and Development Reports RDR–64–5, 15. 1965.

CASSERLY, P. L. "What College Students Say About Advanced Placement—Part I." *College Board Review*, 1968 (69), 6–10.

CASSERLY, P. L., PETERSON, R. E., AND COFFMAN, W. E. *An Interview Survey of Advanced Placement Policies and Practices at Sixty-three Colleges—Part II*. Princeton: Educational Testing Service, Research and Development Reports RDR–64–5, No. 15, 1965.

CHAMBERLIN, D. and others. *Did They Succeed in College?*, Vol. IV. New York: Harper and Row, 1942.

CHICKERING, A. W. *Education and Identity*. San Francisco: Jossey-Bass, 1969.

CHRIST-JANER, A. F. "Credit by Examination." In D. W. Vermilye (Ed.), *The Expanded Campus: Current Issues in Higher Education 1972*. San Francisco: Jossey-Bass, 1972.

College Entrance Examination Board. *College Credit by Examination Through the College-Level Examination Program*. Princeton, 1970.

College Entrance Examination Board. *A Guide to the Advanced Placement Program, 1967–1968*. New York, 1967.

COMMANGER, H. W., MC EWEN, R. W., AND BLANCHARD, B. *Education in a Free Society*. Pittsburgh: University of Pittsburgh Press, 1960.

Commission on Non-Traditional Study. *New Dimensions for the Learner*. New York, 1971.

CROSS, K. P. "On Creativity." *The Research Reporter*, 1967, *II*, 1–4.

CROSS, K. P. "New Students of the '70's." *The Research Reporter*, 1971, *VI* (4), 1–5.

CURETON, L. W. "The History of Grading Practices." *Measurement in Education*, 1971, *2* (4), 1–8.

References

DAVAGE, R. H. *Summary of Two Pyramid Project Experiments in Meteorology 300—TV, 1958–59.* University Park: Division of Academic Research and Services, Pennsylvania State University, 1959.

DAVIS, J. A. *Great Aspirations.* Chicago: Aldine, 1964.

DRESSEL, P. L. *Evaluation in Higher Education.* Boston: Houghton-Mifflin, 1961.

DRESSEL, P. L., (Ed.) *The New Colleges: Toward an Appraisal.* Iowa City: The American College Testing Program, 1971.

DUBIN, R., AND BEISSE, F. "The Assistant: Academic Subaltern." *Administrative Science Quarterly,* 1966–1967, *2,* 521–47.

DUBIN, R., AND TAVEGGIA, T. C. *The Teaching-Learning Paradox.* Eugene: Center for the Advanced Study of Educational Administration, University of Oregon, 1968.

DYKES, A. R. *Faculty Participation in Academic Decision Making.* Washington: American Council on Education, 1968.

ELBOW, P. H. "More Accurate Evaluation of Student Performance." *The Journal of Higher Education,* 1969, *40,* 219–230.

Empire State College. *Bulletin, 1971–72.* Saratoga Springs, New York, 1971.

ERHART, R. R. *Audio-Tutorial Instruction in Physical Geography.* Kalamazoo: Western Michigan University, n.d.

ERICKSEN, S. C. "Grading ≠ Evaluation." In *Memo to the Faculty,* 46. Ann Arbor: Center for Research on Learning and Teaching, University of Michigan, 1971.

ERICKSEN, S. C. "Teaching Fellows." In *Memo to the Faculty,* 13. Ann Arbor: Center for Research on Learning and Teaching, University of Michigan, 1965.

EURICH, A. D. *"Better Instruction with Fewer Teachers."* In G. K. Smith (Ed.), *Current Issues in Higher Education, 1956.* Washington: Association for Higher Education, 1956, 10–16.

EURICH, N., AND SCHWENKMEYER, B. *Great Britain's Open University: First Chance, Second Chance, or Last Chance?* New York: Academy for Educational Development, 1971.

References

EVANS, R. I. *Resistance to Innovation in Higher Education.* San Francisco: Jossey-Bass, 1968.

EVANS, R. I., SMITH, R. G., AND COLVILLE, W. K. *The University Faculty and Educational Television: Hostility, Resistance, and Change.* Grant 741015, USOE. Houston: University of Houston, 1962.

Evergreen State College. *Bulletin 1971–72.* Olympia, Washington: Evergreen State College, 1971.

Experiment on Independent Study, 1957–58. Yellow Springs, Ohio: Antioch College, 1958.

FAGIN, M. C. "CLEP Credit Encourages Adults to Seek Degrees." *College Board Review,* 1971 (81), 18–22.

FASHING, J., AND DEUTSCH, S. E. *Academics in Retreat.* Albuquerque: University of New Mexico Press, 1971.

FELDMAN, K. A., AND NEWCOMB, T. M. *The Impact of College on Students.* San Francisco: Jossey-Bass, 1969.

FINGER, F. W. "Professional Problems: Preparation for a Career in College Teaching." *American Psychologist,* 1969, *24,* 1044–1049.

FISCHER, J. "Survival U is Alive and Burgeoning in Green Bay, Wisconsin." *Harpers,* 1971, *242*(1449), 20–27.

FOWLER, T. (Ed.) *Locke's Conduct of the Understanding.* New York: Macmillan, 1890.

FRANKEL, C. *Issues in University Education.* New York: Harper and Row, 1959.

Fund for the Advancement of Education. *They Went to College Early.* New York, 1957.

GAFF, J. G. and associates. *The Cluster College.* San Francisco: Jossey-Bass, 1970.

GARDNER, J. W. *The Pursuit of Excellence: Education and the Future of America.* New York: Doubleday, 1958.

GREEN, B. A., JR. *Is the Keller Plan Catching On Too Fast?* Cambridge: Education Research Center, Massachusetts Institute of Technology, 1971.

GREENSPOON, J. Associate Dean of Faculty, Temple Buell College, Denver. Letter to author, December 17, 1971.

GRUBER, H. E., AND WEITMAN, M. *Self-Directed Study: Experiments in Higher Education.* Boulder, Colo.: University of Colorado, Behavior Research Laboratory Report No. 19, 1962.

HARRIS, J. W. "Baccalaureate Requirements: Attainments or Exposures?" *Educational Record,* 1972, *53*(1), 59–65.

HARTLEY, E. L. Dean for Educational Development, University of Wisconsin, Green Bay. Letter to author, February 16, 1972a.

HARTLEY, E. L. Dean for Educational Development, University of Wisconsin, Green Bay. Letter to author, February 26, 1972b.

HEFFERLIN, JB L. *Dynamics of Academic Reform.* San Francisco: Jossey-Bass, 1969.

HEIST, P., AND BILORUSKY, J. "A Special Breed of Students." In J. G. Gaff and associates (Eds.), *The Cluster College.* San Francisco: Jossey-Bass, 1970.

HODGKINSON, H. L. "Governance and Factions: Who Decides Who Decides?" *The Research Reporter,* 1968, *3,* 4–7.

HODGKINSON, H. L., WALTER, W., AND COOVER, R. "Bard Corrects Freshmen Themes on Tape." *AAHE College and University Bulletin,* 1968, *20*(10), 2–3.

HOFSTADTER, R. *Anti-Intellectualism in American Life.* New York: Vintage Books, 1966.

HOLLAND, J. L. "Undergraduate Origins of American Scientists." *Science,* 1957, *126,* 433–437.

HOYT, D. P. *The Relationship Between College Grades and Adult Achievement.* Iowa City: American College Testing Program, 1965.

HUTCHINS, R. M. *The Higher Learning in America.* New Haven: Yale University Press, 1936.

HUTCHISON, W. R. "Yes, John, There are Teachers on the Faculty." In O. Milton and E. J. Shoben, Jr. (Eds.) *Learning and the Professors.* Athens, Ohio: Ohio University Press, 1968, 36–48.

ILLICH, I. *Deschooling Society.* New York: Harper and Row, 1971a.

ILLICH, I. "Education: A Consumer Commodity and a Pseudo-

References

Religion." *The Christian Century,* 1971b, *88*(50), 1464–1468.

JACOB, P. E. *Changing Values in College.* New Haven: Edward W. Hazen Foundation, 1956.

JACOBSON, R. L. "National External Degree Explored by College Board." *The Chronicle of Higher Education,* 1972, *6* (22), 6.

JENCKS, C., AND RIESMAN, D. *The Academic Revolution.* New York: Doubleday, 1968.

JENNINGS, W. N. *Assessment of Instructor Differences Using the Word-Association Examination.* Knoxville, Tenn. University Microfilm 69–7163, 1968.

KELLER, F. S. "Good-bye, Teacher." *Journal of Applied Behavior Analysis,* 1968, *1*(1), 79–89.

KELLER, F. S. "A Personal Course in Psychology." In Roger Ulrich, Thomas Stachnik, and John Mabry (Eds.), *Control of Human Behavior.* Glenview, Illinois: Scott, Foresman, 1966.

KELLER, F. S. "Something Like It, Part 2." *Personalized System of Instruction Newsletter,* 1971 (2), 1–2.

KESTIN, J. "Reflections on the Teaching of Engineering at a University." *American Scientist,* 1963, *51,* 437.

KITZHABER, A. R. *Themes, Theories, and Therapy: The Teaching of Writing in College.* New York: McGraw-Hill, 1963.

KNAPP, R. H., AND GOODRICH, H. B. *Origins of American Scientists.* Chicago: University of Chicago Press, 1952.

KOEN, F. M. *State of the Program Report: Michigan College Teacher Training Program.* Ann Arbor: University of Michigan, 1969.

KOEN, F., AND ERICKSEN, S. *An Analysis of the Specific Features which Characterize the More Successful Programs for the Recruitment and Training of College Teachers.* Final Report, Project S–482. USOE. Ann Arbor: University of Michigan, The Center for Research on Learning and Teaching, 1967.

KORN, J. H. "Promoting Good Teaching." *Journal of Higher Education,* 1972, *43*(2), 123–132.

References

KURTZ, E. J. "Process Approach in Biology Instruction." Paper presented at annual meeting of the Entomological Society of America, Dallas, December, 1968.

LADD, D. R. *Change in Educational Policy: Self-Studies in Selected Colleges and Universities.* New York: McGraw-Hill, 1970.

LEARNED, W. S., AND WOOD, B. D. *The Student and his Knowledge.* New York: Carnegie Foundation, 1938.

LINDENMEYER, R. S. "A Comparison Study of the Academic Progress of the Cooperative and the Four-Year Student." *Journal of Cooperative Education,* 1967, *3*(2), 8–18.

LINDQUIST, E. F. *A First Course in Statistics: Their Use and Interpretation in Education and Psychology.* Boston: Houghton Mifflin, 1942.

MACOMBER, F. G. (Ed.) *Experimental Study in Instructional Procedures.* Oxford, Ohio: Miami University, 1957.

MAGUIRE, J. D. "Strategies for Academic Reform." In H. L. Hodgkinson and M. B. Bloy, Jr. (Eds.) *Identity Crisis in Higher Education.* San Francisco: Jossey-Bass, 1971, 92–112.

MAIER, N. R. F. "Innovation in Education." *American Psychologist,* 1971, *26*(8), 722–725.

MARTIN, W. B. "The Relevance of Present Educational Systems." *The Research Reporter,* 1971a, *4*(2), 4–5.

MARTIN, W. B. "Thoughts on Evaluation and Imagination." In P. L. Dressel (Ed.), *The New Colleges: Toward an Appraisal.* Iowa City: American College Testing Program, 1971b.

MARTIN, W. B. "To Whom is the University Responsible—and for What?" *Notes from DIRS,* 1971c, *4*(1), 2–12.

MC CANN, C. J. "Vital Undergraduate Studies: What's the Right Climate?" Paper presented at the meeting of the WICHE Institute of Departmental and Institutional Development, Lake Arrowhead, California, 1969.

MC CONNELL, T. R., AND HEIST, P. A. "Do Students Make the College?" *College and University,* 1959, *35*, 442–452.

MC KEACHIE, W. J. *Research on College Teaching: A Review.*

References

Washington, D.C.: ERIC Clearing House on Higher Education, 1970.

MEYER, G. "An Experimental Study of the Old and New Types of Examination." *Journal of Educational Psychology,* 1935, *26,* 30–40.

MILLER, R. I. *Evaluating Faculty Performance.* San Francisco: Jossey-Bass, 1972.

MILLER, S. *Measure, Number, and Weight: A Polemical Statement of the College Grading Problem.* Berkeley: Select Committee on Education of the University of California at Berkeley, 1966.

MILTON, O. *"Patris Potestatis."* *Teaching-Learning Issues,* 1970, *13,* 1–12.

MILTON, O. "Learning Transfer." *Teaching-Learning Issues,* 1971, *15,* 1–11.

MONROE, P. *Source Book of the History of Education for the Greek and Roman Period.* London: Macmillan, 1902.

MOONEY, R. L. "The Problem of Leadership in the University." *Harvard Educational Review,* 1963, *33,* 42–57.

MORISON, E. E. "A Case Study of Innovation." In W. G. Bennis, K. D. Benne, and R. Chin (Eds.) *The Planning of Change: Readings in the Applied Behavioral Sciences.* New York: Holt, Rinehart, and Winston, 1961, 592–605.

MUNN, N. L. Cited in *Introduction to Psychology.* Boston: Houghton Mifflin, 1962.

NEWMAN, F. *Report on Higher Education.* Washington, D.C.: Government Printing Office, 1971.

NOWLIS, V., CLARK, K. E., AND ROCK, M. *The Graduate Student as Teacher.* Washington: American Council on Education, 1968.

O'NEILL, J. *Resource Use in Higher Education.* New York: Carnegie Commission, 1971.

OLSON, W. E. *A Report to the College.* Rohnert Park, California: Sonoma State College, 1971.

PACE, C. R. "Perspectives on the Student and his College." In L. E. Dennis and J. F. Kauffman (Eds.) *The College and the*

Student. Washington, D.C.: American Council on Education, 1966.

PACE, C. R. AND MILNE, M. "College Graduates: Highlights from a Nationwide Survey." *Evaluation Comment,* 1971, *3*(2), 1–7.

PACE, C. R. and staff. *Higher Education Measurement and Evaluation Kit*. Los Angeles: Center for the Study of Evaluation, University of California, 1971.

PLANT, W. T. "Longitudinal Changes in Intolerance and Authoritarianism for Subjects Differing in Amount of College Education over Four Years." *Genetic Psychology Monographs,* 1965, *72,* 247–287.

PLANT, W. T. *Personality Changes Associated with a College Education*. San Jose, California: San Jose State College, 1962.

POSTLETHWAIT, S. W., NOVAK, J., AND MURRAY, H. *An Integrated Experience Approach to Learning*. Minneapolis: Burgess, 1964.

PRESSEY, S. L. " 'Fordling' Accelerates Ten Years After." *Journal of Counseling Psychology,* 1967, *14*(1), 73–80.

PRESSEY, S. L. "Two Basic Neglected Psychoeducational Problems." *American Psychologist,* 1965, *20*(6), 391–395.

RAIMI, R. A. "Examinations and Grades in College." *AAUP Bulletin,* 1967, 309–317.

RICHARD, J. "The Good Man." *Change,* 1971, *3*(6), 5ff.

RODES, H. P. "The After Effects of Cooperative Education." *Journal of Cooperative Education,* 1968, *4*(2), 13–23.

RUST, J. D. "The Ombudsman Office at Michigan State University." In S. V. Anderson (Ed.) *Ombudsman Papers: American Experience and Proposals*. Berkeley: Institute of Governmental Studies, University of California, 1969, 321–336.

SHAW, W. B. *Senior Student Perceptions of Justin Morrill College: Observations on the Achievement of the College Goals, Class of 1969*. East Lansing: Justin Morrill College, Michigan State University, 1970.

SHOBEN, E. J. JR. Executive Vice-president, Evergreen State Col-

References

lege, Olympia, Washington. Letter to author, November 12, 1971.

SIEGEL, L. "The Contributions and Implications of Recent Research Related to Improving Teaching and Learning." In O. Milton and E. J. Shoben, Jr. (Eds.) *Learning and the Professors.* Athens, Ohio: Ohio University Press, 1968, 136–157.

SMITH, V. B. "College Finances: Ills and Remedies." *Research Report,* 4. Washington: American Association for Higher Education, 1971.

STETSON, R. F. "Getting a Head Start on College." *College Board Review,* 1971 (81), 23–25.

STRONG, F. Dean of Freshmen, California Institute of Technology, Pasadena, California. Letter to author, March 7, 1967.

SUTTON, J. T., and ALLEN, E. D. *The Effect of Practice and Evaluation on Improvement in Written Composition.* Cooperative Research Project 1993, USOE. Deland, Florida: Stetson University, 1964.

SWEET, D. E. "Innovations in Undergraduate Learning." Paper presented at the meeting of the American Association for Higher Education, Chicago, 1972.

TERMAN, L. M. "Discovery and Encouragement of Exceptional Talent." *American Psychologist,* 1954, *9*(6), 221–230.

THISTLETHWAITE, D. L. "College Environments and the Development of Talent." *Science,* 1959, *130*, 71–76.

THOMAS, L., and AUGSTEIN, S. *An Experimental Approach to Learning from Written Material.* Uxbridge, England: Centre for the Study of Human Learning, Brunel University, 1970.

TRENT, J. W. and MEDSKER, L. L. *Beyond High School.* San Francisco: Jossey-Bass, 1968.

TROUTT, R. *Special Degree Programs for Adults: Exploring Nontraditional Degree Programs in Higher Education.* Iowa City: American College Testing Program, 1971.

TYLER, R. W. "Values and Objectives." In Asa S. Knowles and associates (Eds.) *Handbook of Cooperative Education.* San Francisco: Jossey-Bass, 1971.

References

University of Alabama. *A College for You: The New College Bulletin.* University, Ala.: University of Alabama, 1970.

University of Wisconsin, Green Bay. *Catalog, 1972–73.* Green Bay, 1972.

WALZ, T. H. *Living-Learning Center: Annual Report, 1970–71.* Minneapolis: The Living-Learning Center, University of Minnesota, 1971.

WARREN, J. R. *College Grading Practices: An Overview.* Washington: ERIC Clearing House on Higher Education, 1971.

WEBB, N. J., AND GRIB, T. F. *Teaching Process as a Learning Experience: The Experimental Use of Student-Led Discussion Groups.* ED 019 708. Bethesda, Maryland: ERIC Document Reproduction Service, National Cash Register Co., 1967.

WILLIAMS, J. E., AND RICHMAN, C. L. "The Graduate Preparation of the College Professor of Psychology: A Survey." *American Psychologist,* 1971, *26*(11), 1000–1009.

WILSON, J. W. "Growth and Current Status of Cooperative Engineering Education." *Engineering Education,* 1971a, *61* (7), 790–794.

WILSON, J. W. "Survey of Cooperative Education, 1971." *Journal of Cooperative Education,* 1971b, *8*(1), 39–51.

WILSON, J. W., AND LYONS, E. H. *Work-Study College Programs: Appraisal and Report of the Study of Cooperative Education. New York:* Harper and Row, 1961.

147

Other Selected Sources

ASTIN, A. W., AND PANOS, R. J. *The Educational and Vocational Development of College Students.* Washington, D.C.: American Council on Education, 1969.

COOK, J. M., AND NEVILLE, R. F. *The Faculty as Teachers: A Perspective on Evaluation.* Bethesda, Maryland: ERIC Document Reproduction Service, 1971. ED 054 392.

CROSS, K. P. *Beyond the Open Door.* San Francisco: Jossey-Bass, 1971.

DRESSEL, P. L., AND DE LISLE, F. H. *Undergraduate Curriculum*

Trends. Washington: American Council on Education, 1969.

DUNHAM, E. A. *Colleges of the Forgotten Americans.* New York: McGraw-Hill, 1969.

GAGNE, R. M. *The Conditions of Learning.* New York: Holt, Rinehart, and Winston, 1965.

HENDERSON, A. D. *The Innovative Spirit.* San Francisco: Jossey-Bass, 1970.

HODGKINSON, H. L. *Institutions in Transition.* New York: McGraw-Hill, 1970.

KELSEY, R. R. *AAHE Bibliography on Higher Education.* Washington: American Association for Higher Education, 1972.

KNOWLES, M. S. *The Modern Practice of Adult Education: Andragogy versus Pedagogy.* New York: Association Press, 1970.

KORN, J. H. "Promoting Good Teaching." Pittsburgh: Carnegie-Mellon University, 1971.

MAYHEW, L. B. *Changing Practices in Education for the Professions.* Atlanta: Southern Regional Education Board, 1971.

MAYHEW, L. B. *Contemporary College Students and the Curriculum.* Atlanta: Southern Regional Education Board, 1969.

MAYHEW, L. B. *Innovation in Collegiate Instruction: Strategies for Change.* Atlanta: Southern Regional Education Board, 1967.

MORRIS, W. H. (Ed.) *Effective College Teaching.* Washington: American Association for Higher Education, 1970.

PACE, C. R. *Thoughts on Evaluation in Higher Education.* Iowa City: American College Testing Program, 1972.

PATTERSON, L. D. *Consortia in American Higher Education.* Bethesda, Maryland: ERIC Document Reproduction Service, 1970. ED 043 800.

ROTHWELL, C. E. *The Importance of Teaching: A Memorandum to the New College Teacher.* New Haven: The Hazen Foundation, 1968.

SHARON, A. T. *College Credit for Off-Campus Study.* Bethesda,

Other Selected Sources

Maryland: ERIC Document Reproduction Service, 1971. ED 048 520.

SMITH, G. K. (Ed.) *The Troubled Campus: Current Issues in Higher Education.* San Francisco: Jossey-Bass, 1970.

SMITH, G. K. (Ed.). *New Teaching, New Learning: Current Issues in Higher Education.* San Francisco: Jossey-Bass, 1971.

SPURR, S. H. *Academic Degree Structures: Innovative Approaches.* New York: McGraw-Hill, 1970.

The Student in Higher Education. New Haven: The Hazen Foundation, 1968.

VALLANCE, T. R. *Structural Innovations in Higher Education to Meet Social Needs.* Bethesda, Maryland: ERIC Document Reproduction Service, 1970. ED 044 539.

WITHEY, S. B., and others. *A Degree and What Else: A Review of the Correlates and Consequences of a College Education.* New York: McGraw-Hill, 1971.

The following research reports (each one approximately fifty pages)) are available at $2.00 per copy from: American Association of Higher Education, One Dupont Circle, Suite 780, Washington, D.C. 20036.

BOWEN, H., *Who Benefits from Higher Education?* 1972.

BREEDIN, B., *Disenchantment of Public with Higher Education,* 1972.

DICKEY, F., *Accreditation Trends,* 1972.

HARVEY, J., *Compendium on Nontraditional Study,* 1972.

SCHOENFELD, J., *Student Role in Curricula Change,* 1972.

TILLERY, D., *Transition of Youth from School to College,* 1972.

WILLINGHAM, W., *Transition of Youth from Community to Four-Year College,* 1972.

Index

151

Index

Index

155

Index